A comprehensive guide
with practical exercises
to the techniques
of display typography

Eric K Bain

The theory and practice of
typographic design

VISUAL COMMUNICATION BOOKS
HASTINGS HOUSE, PUBLISHERS
10 East 40th Street, New York, N.Y. 10016

Printed and bound in Great Britain
by W. & J. Mackay & Co. Ltd, Chatham, Kent

contents

The author wishes to express his gratitude
to all those who have granted their
permission to reproduce the samples of
print contained in this book.

about this book

It is the purpose of this work to present, in practical and easily assimilable
form, the principles which underlie display typography. The information and
skills to be learned are arranged in a logical sequence which conducts the
reader step by step from the most elementary to advanced levels of technique.

For students of typographic design and others who intend to practise
typography numerous exercises are provided. These are in every case carefully constructed to test the student's understanding of the content of the
relevant section. All the exercises have been previously tested with students
in simulated conditions and the results have proved satisfactory, but it must
be emphasised that expert personal advice and constructive criticism of the
completed exercises are still essential to the reader who aims at a professional
degree of proficiency.

This book is intended for those who wish to acquire a critical appreciation
of typography without necessarily practising it, and for already competent
typographers who are looking for a rational framework for their work which
would lead to a deeper understanding of basic principles and therefore
greater freedom and more originality in creation. With this in mind, the text
is written so that it can be read as a whole without reference to practical work.

Any attempt to cover the entire field of typographic design in all its
aspects and with the depth and thoroughness of the present work would run
to many volumes. Therefore, where information subsidiary to the main purpose of the book is readily available elsewhere, reference is made to the source.
Thus duplication of much information which is already accessible is avoided.
An extensive bibliography for further study is appended, so that specialist
interests can be pursued.

The approach to the subject is in some ways novel in that it does not treat
design as an end in itself. Unfortunately, the design of print is often taught as
if it were merely a subdivision of general design as offered in art schools. In
fact, it more properly belongs to the field of communication. Certainly, it
employs form, colour and other elements of the visual arts, but only in a
capacity subsidiary to the main purpose, which remains the communication
of ideas by means of printed words and pictures. In this book, therefore, the
emphasis from the first is properly placed on effective mass communication,
only secondarily on 'design' in the restricted sense of the creation of an
aesthetically satisfying decorated surface. Accordingly, the work begins with
a discussion on the nature and purpose of typographic design, while the
sections immediately following explore the crucial relationship between the
logic of the printed word and its aesthetics.

Any treatment of basic principles in design must tend to oversimplify in the interest of clarity. It would be a pity, however, if any reader should form the impression from the following pages that there exists sets of inflexible rules which govern the appearance of print. As long as the aims of typography are grasped, it should become apparent once the latter parts of the book are reached that, according to circumstances, any 'rule' is capable of being profitably broken.

But the student who deduces from an examination of well-designed print that there are no rules at all, and who does not consider it worth his while to acquaint himself with the principles of typography, is unlikely to produce consistently good work. Such a student is likely to rely heavily on imitating the work of others, most probably the examples illustrated in the many glossy collections of current graphics.

Too complete a reliance on such illustrations can be misleading in other ways. The work shown is often chosen from a restricted and unrepresentative range of high-status print, with little immediate relevance to the everyday work of the majority of practising designers. An attempt has been made here to redress the balance, by introducing and including exercises on the less glamorous but equally essential parts of the typographer's trade. The illustrations of printed specimens have been selected because each demonstrates a successful solution to a particular design problem, while at the same time explaining visually the text which accompanies it. They are not intended to make up a gallery of ready-made cribs, nor is it the purpose of the many diagrams to lend themselves to thoughtless imitation.

It is intended too that study of this book will prove of benefit to those who are mainly concerned with the commissioning of designs, in that only a thorough knowledge of principles will enable them to discriminate between the reasoned, sound layout and the superficial and derivative.

materials needed

Working layouts are drawn in pencil on translucent paper. While a single HB is enough for the earlier exercises, from section 10 one harder and one softer pencil will prove useful. Any thin, white bank paper is suitable for layouts, and can be bought from an artists' supplier or printer in pads or sheets. When colour is introduced in section 17 coloured pencils are required. Either then or later, when realistic visuals are attempted, good designers' colours and brushes should be acquired. With these a high white matt cartridge with enough substance to reduce buckling is necessary.

In section 41 various other media are suggested: felt- and fibre-tipped pens, transfer colour, film and coloured tissue. As finished layouts for customer submission are not asked for, drawing instruments such as are described in Garland: *Graphics handbook* are not needed, but the practising typographer will want to have them in any case. Ball-point and evenline pens are unsuited to the preparation of working layouts and roughs.

A type scale, preferably steel, is required from the start. A scale from which conversions between millimetres and 12pt ems can be made at a glance is preferable. One such is manufactured by Rabone Chesterman to a PIRA design. Also useful is the British Federation of Master Printer's metric conversion calculator. Copyfitting tables are available from Monotype and Linotype and are incorporated in the type specimen sheets issued by Intertype. A PPE typographic slide rule can speed up copyfitting considerably. For section 31 and after, a Monotype keyboard operator's set-em scale is an optional extra.

Type specimens can be had from various sources, the Monotype series of students' sheets being especially useful. For the first dozen sections only a few text types, carefully selected to provide variety with maximum flexibility in use, are recommended. Bembo or Garamond, together with Baskerville or Imprint, might form a sound basis, while Plantin or Ehrhardt would answer the occasional need for a sturdier face, as when printing on coated stock. A modern such as Walbaum or Bodoni with its respective bold would complete the range. Note that, particularly in text sizes, subtle variations go unnoticed and there are far too many type designs on the market today which are all too similar in appearance even to the expert. A good typographer does not need a wide selection of typefaces.

Section 13 calls for specimen sheets of display faces. Choose from the vast range available the minimum which will suffice for normal occasions. Exclude for the moment, however exciting they may look, types which are too distinctive in cut to be of more than limited use, such as three-dimensional and highly decorative letters. With experience the student will come to rely less on novelty for providing interest in his typographic layout. Variation in weight, width and style are the main requirements in the selection of a compact yet versatile range. The larger sizes, particularly the bold, of some text faces such as Walbaum and Perpetua make excellent display lines. Specimen sheets of sanserif are called for in section 26. On grounds of availability, design and range of related founts, Monotype Univers has much to commend it.

Type specimen sheets for line composition, required in section 32, are more difficult to come by. Those issued by the companies are more in the nature of advertisements than of value to typographers. The same is true of foundry type specimen sheets. No such difficulty arises in the case of rules, borders and ornaments, a variety of which can be inspected in any specimen book. Alternatively, the manufacturer will supply sheets on demand.

When colour is introduced later, it would be advisable to have at hand some ink manufacturers' sample books. Some of these, such as Fishbourne's *Colorchart*, show a wide range of tints and shades as well as the basic ink colours. They are well worth acquiring. As many paper samples from merchants and manufacturers as possible should be also collected.

The meaning of unfamiliar terms appearing in the text may be found in Glaister: *The glossary of the book.*

In as many cases as possible, the student's completed layout should be set up and proofed exactly as indicated, then minor adjustments made to the design and the final proof filed away with the layout. Where facilities for printing do not exist the student is at a serious disadvantage, because he has no way of checking the accuracy of his specifications or seeing the effect of the finished job.

1 the nature of typographic design

The written word, aided by both autographic and photographic images, is still today our most important method of communication, despite competition from relatively recent inventions such as telephone, telegraph, radio and television. Written language has several main advantages. Like these other media, though not so instantaneously, it can be easily transported over distances. Unlike them, it can deliver its message continuously over a period of time and is capable through printing of being mass-produced.

speech into print

The translation of speech into writing entails a loss. Vocal inflexions, facial expressions and gestures, on which we rely so much for interpreting speech, are eliminated. One of the objects of design in printing is to compensate for this loss by organizing the visual properties of the printed word so as to communicate the message to the reader with the greatest possible efficiency. A factor unique to the written or printed word is that the page can be scanned and the organization of the information understood before reading. Personal selection of what is relevant to the reader becomes possible, which is not the case with those media which are aural rather than visual, instantaneous instead of continuous.

author
|
printer and designer
|
reader

Printing is a means of mass-producing identical visually conveyed messages. The printer's business is to take a message originated by an author and reproduce it in quantity so that it can be disseminated to a large number of readers. To increase the effectiveness of the message the printer calls on the designer to help, either indirectly as the designer of the types he uses or directly through the services of an artist, graphic designer or typographer. Thus design in printing can be seen to be primarily an aid to communication.

optics and conventions

The effectiveness of a piece of print as communication depends on three factors, each controlled by the designer. To begin with, the printed image must be both visible and legible. Visibility is attained by working within the limitations of the human eye. The relationship between reading distance and type size, and the tonal contrast required between image and background, are typical instances. Legibility includes visibility but is also a matter of observing conventions. The letter shapes which have been developed for printing types are, like the alphabet itself, artificial and arbitrary, having no connection with meaning. Left-to-right reading, word spaces, punctuation and paragraphing are likewise conventions of writing. A knowledge of the capabilities of the eye and of the conventions which compose the printed word are therefore primary requisites of the designer.

pictures

The second factor in effective communication is the pictorial element. This book concentrates on the type component in print, but modern production techniques and the increasing public acceptance of pictorial communication, as in television, are causing more emphasis to be placed on pictures, with correspondingly less reliance on the printed word. In practice the typographer is responsible for the deployment, if not the creation of pictures and this is dealt with in the final chapters.

form and colour The third factor is the formal elements such as shape and colour. These constitute a distinct and self-sufficient language in themselves, without the help of words and if need be, without pictorial representation. As used by the artist, this language is more capable of communicating subtle yet precise feelings than is everyday speech or writing. Unlike the process of reading, perception of form and colour is instantaneous, which makes them suitable for certain factual, informative purposes also, such as maps and diagrams. 13

communication Form and colour have meaning for us: different shapes and colours arouse in us specific responses which, although they can be refined and intensified by training, are broadly the same for everyone. So we can claim that these formal abstract elements comprise a language with a vocabulary and grammar of its own, which can be made use of by the designer of print to help communicate ideas. It is relevant to point out that this language of shape and colour is natural, in direct contact with the world of the senses, not arbitrary and conventional like speech and writing. Much of its immediacy and strength of appeal must be due to this fact. There is however a difference between the ways in which the artist and the designer use this language. While the artist is concerned with self-expression, the designer tries to express the message which originated with the author—the printer's client. In brief, the designer must plan the appearance of print to achieve a fusion of all three factors—legibility, pictorial content and formal qualities—into an effective statement of the client's message.

status Form and colour lend status to a piece of print. Before the industrial revolution, the expensiveness at hand-made materials and manual methods of production automatically made printed works valued. For this reason and also because of the limited needs of society at that time, output was mostly confined to books. Mechanization led to more and cheaper print and changing social conditions called for new kinds of printed product, much of it ephemeral. In the process the status of the printed word became devalued, until today most print is quickly expendable and our eyes practise an unconscious censorship on the mass of material which bombards us. To aggravate the situation, advertising created competitive print, which led first to the emergence of novel, high-impact display faces and then to the arrangement of the type on the paper in non-traditional ways, in efforts to compete for the attention of the public.

Faced today with the problem of communicating via a medium which is held in no special esteem by the public, the designer's use of form and colour is more than ever essential. It enhances the status of the piece of print, and gives the message a greater chance of being noticed, read and believed.

planning A further aspect of print design is the planning of materials used and methods of manufacture, corresponding to the work of the draughtsman in other industries. Paper and ink, methods of composition, printing and binding are important forces which shape the finished product. In each case economic considerations bulk large. The working layout is in fact a blueprint for production and as new management techniques transform the industry, it can be expected to become a normal and indispensable part of the production line.

social responsibility Communication through printing has an important role in society that must be filled with minimum expenditure of materials, time and effort. But there are other obligations to society, less apparent perhaps but no less important. Just as an architect has not only a responsibility to his client to provide a building which satisfies his requirements, but has also a duty to the community to erect a structure which improves the environment, so the designer of print must uphold aesthetic standards in all he undertakes. If we believe that the quality of our visual environment has influence for good or bad on the quality of life we lead, then it must be recognized that print forms an extensive part of this environment and deserves our most creative and imaginative efforts.

fashion Fashion has a significant place in design. Whenever a piece of print has to belong visibly to a particular period, whether some time in the historical past or, more usually, the up-to-the-minute present, the style associated with that period must be used. Fashions reflect the life and ideas of their times, and so the contemporary visual language dictates to a great extent the appearance of print today.

2 symmetrical display

From the early printers until quite recently it was taken for granted that the natural way to display type was to centre each line on the measure. The resulting symmetrical effect is satisfying at a deep level of human consciousness and there is the advantage that type can easily be set in this way by hand and machine. Note that centring of lines is difficult with handwriting or typewriter and therefore differentiates print from these lower status methods of communication. Layouts with centred lines create a feeling of permanence, stability and authority as well as, by association, of tradition.

The reform of typographic design in this century began with the belief that traditional craft standards as practised and handed on by the old printers had degenerated as a result of the social and technological changes introduced during the industrial revolution. Thus the task of improving on low nineteenth-century standards was seen as a rediscovery of sound earlier practices. This revival was in fact carried out, by the amateurs of the private press movement, by the mechanical composing companies and by a few enterprising printers and publishers.

Though it has long since become clear that a revival of styles of the past, based as they are on the book, is in itself inadequate to meet the new demands of today, an understanding of traditional principles of display typography is still of first importance. Accordingly, sections 3 to 20 are devoted to these and the student should not depart from symmetrical principles until the sections on asymmetry are reached.

Title pages by the Foulis Brothers 1750 and by Walter Lewis for Douglas Cleverdon 1929

C. JULII
CAESARIS
ET
A. HIRTII
DE
REBUS A CAESARE GESTIS
COMMENTARII.
CUM FRAGMENTIS.
EX RECENSIONE SAMUELIS CLARKE
FIDELITER EXPRESSI.
VOL. III.

GLASGUAE:
IN AEDIBUS ACADEMICIS
EXCUDEBANT ROB. ET AND. FOULIS
ACADEMIAE TYPOGRAPHI
MDCCL.

GEORGE FARQUHAR
THE BEAUX STRATAGEM
A COMEDY

With Seven Engravings on Copper by
J. E. LABOUREUR
and an Introduction by
BONAMY DOBRÉE

DOUGLAS CLEVERDON
BRISTOL
1929

It often happens when a piece of copy has to be placed on the paper that its length is too great for the width available and it has to be divided into two or more consecutive lines of type. As the purpose of typographic design is to help the reader to understand the wording, the breaks must be made in the most logical and grammatical places.

Usually there is at least one key word—noun, verb, adjective or adverb as opposed to conjunctions, prepositions, pronouns and such of lesser importance—in every line. An unimportant word must not be given undue prominence by placing it in a line by itself. Rather it should accompany its grammatically related key word.

Consider the case of the title 'Printing and the mind of man', which has to be divided into three lines. 'Printing', 'mind' and 'man' are the key words. 'And the' belongs to 'mind', while 'of' is related to 'man'. Therefore 'Printing/and the mind/of man' satisfies the demands of logic better than any other possible division. Note that 'Printing/and/the mind of man', though grammatical, is less acceptable because the unimportant word 'and' is given undeserved prominence by its isolation. However, should a fourth line become required, 'Printing/and/the mind/of man' is the only sensible arrangement. Here 'and' is not objectionably overemphasized because no line contains more than a couple of short words.

Split each of the following titles into *three* lines:
A short history of Indian architecture
A psychological study of typography
The print user's guide to colour
Theory and design in the first machine age

Split each of the following into *four* lines:
Finer points in the spacing and arrangement of type
An invitation to an exhibition of students' work

Split the following into *five* lines:
Now is the time for all good men to come to the aid of the party

PRINTING
AND THE MIND
OF MAN

4 shapes

Typographic design seeks to use form as an expressive element. The predominant visual impression of a line of type is of two horizontal parallel lines, thus:

~~A LINE OF TYPE~~   ~~A line of type~~

The beginning and end of the line are also noticeable features which become more marked as soon as there are a number of consecutive type lines. In such cases the eye tends to connect up the line ends and we become aware of the overall shape formed by the whole group. This phenomenon is of absolutely vital concern to the typographer and is the basis of form in typography. In the examples below, straight lines and curves can easily be seen:

Hoxhoh xohxh ox hoxhxox xohx
  xoh hxoxhxoxh xoxh x
    xoxhx xhxoox
     hoxh

Hoxhoh xohxh ox hoxxhox xohx
  xoh hxoxhxoxh xoxh xoh
    xoxh xh oxhoxx
     oxh

Hoxhoh xohxh ox hoxhxox xohx
xoh hxoxhxoxh xoxh x
xoxhx xhxoox
hoxh

Hoxhoh xohxh ox hoxxhox xohx
xoh hxoxhxoxh xoxh xoh
xoxh xh oxhoxx
oxh

The expert typographer readily selects from the logical possibilities inherent in the copy those shapes which suit his purpose best, but for the moment it is advisable to become acquainted with some rough rules which sort out pleasing from unpleasant shapes. In general, apparent curves are better than straight lines or mixtures of straight and curved. Curves are more natural, less rigid and, indeed, they occur most frequently. Spaces between words or letters should not be visibly interfered with for the sake of the group shape. Additionally, the main weight of a group of lines should be concentrated above the halfway mark to avoid a bottom-heavy, drooping effect. Compare the pleasant formations on the left with the unsatisfactory shapes on the right.

Very long lines should not alternate with very short: the illusion of overall shape is weakened or lost and readability is also impaired (below left). Two lines of equal length in a group suggest a special connection between their meanings. Moreover the verticals formed at their ends are stronger than the shape of the whole group and should be avoided (below right):

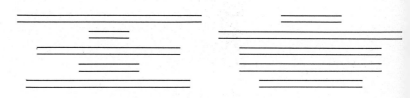

Let us suppose that we wish to divide, logically and by shape, the title 'A study of fine typography through five centuries'. According to the principles outlined in the previous section, the solution would be:

A STUDY
OF FINE TYPOGRAPHY
THROUGH FIVE CENTURIES

But this produces a shape which is unsatisfactory by the standards now suggested. The answer must therefore be *a compromise between the needs of logic and form:*

A STUDY
OF FINE TYPOGRAPHY
THROUGH
FIVE CENTURIES

This early we discover that typographic layout is a matter of making necessary compromises between conflicting demands, particularly between those of sense and shape. Now return to the exercise at the end of the previous section and adjust the line divisions there wherever necessary to form an acceptable shape for each group.

T. E. LAWRENCE

SEVEN
PILLARS OF
WISDOM

A TRIUMPH

1965

EDUCO PRESS · OXFORD

INTRODUCTION

FOUNDATIONS
OF REVOLT

Chapters I to VII

20

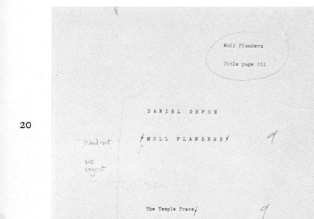

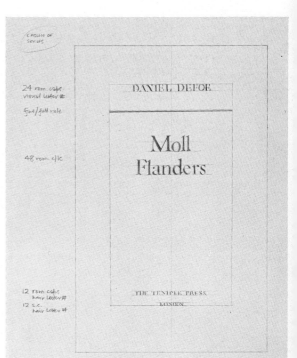

Fully marked-up copy
and working layout
for a title page

DANIEL DEFOE

Moll
Flanders

THE TEMPLE PRESS
LONDON

5 preparing a working layout

A working layout is a blueprint for production, containing visual and written instructions governing the visual elements of a printed job. A highly realistic finish, such as is appropriate in a layout for submission to a customer, is out of place and uneconomic, but absolute accuracy of line length and position together with a full and unambiguous specification of types used and points of style are essential.

A working layout is drawn on thin, tough paper such as bank, which allows tracings to be made from type specimen sheets but can stand up to repeated handling in production departments. Also required is a type scale, preferably steel. Begin by drawing the given size of the job in the middle of the layout paper.

Let us suppose that we wish to use lowercase with initial capitals. The first question is: which words should begin with capital letters? This is a matter of convention, but in this case convention is in a state of transition, presenting us with three alternatives. The 'all-up' style with a capital at every word is archaic and should not be used. The 'all-down' style as printed in the question is too recent a fashion for indiscriminate use. Taking into account the nature of the copy here, an acceptable style would be the insertion of capitals at important words only. Compare:

A History Of The Old English Letter Foundries

A history of the old English letter foundries

A History of the Old English Letter Foundries

Choice of type size is dependent on two main factors: reading distance and degree of impact required. The title on a catalogue cover should be comfortably readable at a distance of rather more than an arm's length and also at normal reading distance, while the purpose of a cover implies bigger type than is used anywhere inside. On the other hand the copy itself does not suggest a very strong treatment. A type body size of around 36pt, depending on the weight and apparent size of the face, seems indicated.

From a specimen sheet choose a normal weight of a roman text face, that is, a type suitable in its smaller sizes for continuous setting, as in bookwork. Avoid related bolds and display faces for the moment. Provisionally decide the number of lines into which the copy is to be split, so that no line is so long as to come uncomfortably near the edges of the paper. Make suitable breaks.

Prepare a working layout for a catalogue cover, size 200 × 125mm (8 × 5 in). *Depth is always quoted first. Inch sizes are approximate.* The copy is: 'A history of the old English letter foundries'.

The next stage is to determine accurately the length each line will make when set. Using the specimen sheet as a guide, mark off every letter width on the edge of a spare sheet of paper, adding appropriate word spacing. Remember that normal space between lowercase words is a thick space, which is one-third of the body height. Do this for each line.

22

specimen sheet

Plantin Monotype

ABCDEFGHIJKLMNOPQR
abcdefghijklmnopqrstuvwxyz

A # H i s t o r y # o f # t h e # O l d # E n g l

spare sheet

Check that the longest line fits nicely within the page width. If not, then the type chosen is too large or too wide in design, or the copy must be broken into more lines.

The type has to be positioned pleasantly on the page. A faint line drawn down the middle of the page area on the layout sheet helps accurate centring of lines. The eye does not accept a mathematical centre as a satisfactory position from top to bottom, however. It greatly prefers a higher situation. A good proportion to observe is two-fifths from the top of the paper, which approximates to the 'Golden Section' of the Greek philosophers. Mark this point on your layout with a faint horizontal line. The group of type lines forming the title will occupy a position extending equally above and below this line. *Note carefully this principle and the proportion used, as it is an important basic fact in design.*

Guide lines the height of the x-height and of the ascenders and descenders can now be lightly indicated on the layout. Using the mark-off of individual letter widths already made on the spare sheet, and tracing through from the specimen sheet, it should be possible to draw each type line in its precise location. In this instance a space of an em or so between lines of type is sufficient to avoid crowding but not so much as to give an impression of disconnected phrases.

This completes the visual instructions. It remains to add the written information in the form of a 'mark-up' which gives precise particulars about type selection and setting. The type series used throughout can be indicated at the top of the layout to avoid repetition. Specifications should be written neatly and legibly at the side of the layout, opposite the line or lines to which they refer but not encroaching on the area representing the paper size of the job.

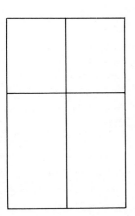

The information requiring to be listed is: *point size* (and body size when this differs from depth of face, eg 10/11pt signifies 10pt type cast on an 11pt body); *style*, whether roman [rom], italic [it], or bold (in the case of some types medium [med] or other terms are used); and *alphabet*, capitals [caps], small capitals [sc], lowercase [lc] or capitals with lowercase [c/lc].

Using the specimen working layouts illustrated on page 20 and below as a guide, complete the mark-up appropriate to the exercise.

23

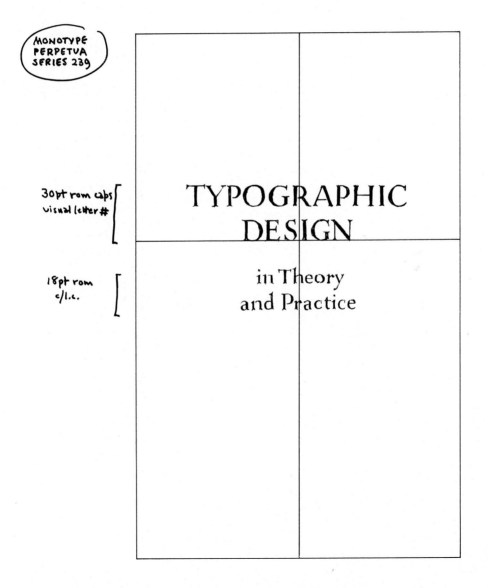

MONOTYPE
PERPETUA
SERIES 239

30pt rom caps
visual letter #

18pt rom
c/l.c.

TYPOGRAPHIC DESIGN

in Theory
and Practice

Let us say that this time we wish to use capitals only. The choice between the two sets of letters is not just one of caprice. It is accepted that capitals look clumsy and lack legibility when set in quantity, but the present copy presents no difficulties in this direction. On the other hand they have a monumental, formal and authoritative character, derived from their inscriptional origin, which is apt for certain purposes.

MINISTRY OF DEFENCE

Lowercase, whether accompanied by initial capitals or not, is less rigid in appearance, more informal and human, and more legible in copy extending to more than a dozen words. A larger point size is of course needed with lowercase to achieve the same apparent size as any line of capitals. Even allowing for this, lowercase is the narrower alphabet while capitals are more economic in depth. Difficulties caused by lines being too long or too short for the given paper width can partly be solved by employing the appropriate alphabet.

Shrewd people today put family capital into Unit Trusts

Italic capitals are not much used together, certainly not in quantity, as there are severe problems in letterspacing and legibility. Italic lowercase is in most founts even more economic in length of line than roman and has a graceful, casual air, the slope imparting a sense of movement. Italic type derives from handwriting.

Hey! you with the car to insure . . .

The preparation of a working layout for this exercise proceeds as before, with some new points to be noted. In type, capitals are designed with the correct space to the side of them to combine well with lowercase when used as initials. When a line is set all in capitals, this space is not enough and it is preferable for reasons of legibility and appearance to add letterspacing. In hand setting text sizes (up to 14pt) the hair space is specified. This applies to small capitals too. For capitals in sizes exceeding 14pt, *visual* letterspacing is better, as described in Dowding: *Finer points in the spacing and arrangement of type*. When marking off letter widths to obtain line length, add a point per character in text sizes, proportionately more in display sizes. The instruction 'hair letterspaced' (hair l/s) or 'visual letterspaced' (visual l/s) must be added to the mark-up for the line, as in the specimen layouts illustrated earlier.

When using three or more consecutive lines of capitals a good effect is achieved if the apparent space between the lines equals the height of the capitals as printed.

The comma in the copy requires to be inserted only if it is to appear within a line. It is visually annoying and adds nothing to the sense of the wording if permitted to stand at the end of a line.

Now proceed to make a working layout of the exercise, taking care to follow the sequence of operations laid down in the previous section.

THE PLAYS OF

EURIPIDES

IN TWO VOLUMES

2

J M DENT AND SONS LIMITED
E P DUTTON AND CO INC

*Painting for
Pleasure*

A STUDENT PAINTER'S HANDBOOK

by R. O. Dunlop

Phoenix House Limited
LONDON

26 Prepare a working layout for a sticker, finished size 100×75mm (4×3in), incorporating the wording: 'All over the world BOAC takes good care of you'. Use normal weight of one text type series only.

When the title to be displayed reaches a certain length it becomes monotonous to set it throughout in the same size of type. In nearly all such copy, certain words or phrases could justifiably be emphasized. The simplest way of doing so, at the same time overcoming the monotony due to lack of variety of scale, is to set this part in a larger size of type.

Another advantage is then gained. Major display groups consisting of identically-set lines dissipate their impact over the entire printed area. Emphasizing a small part of such a group provides a focal point and concentrates the reader's attention. Compare:

A psychological
study
of typography

A psychological
study of
typography

Nineteenth century
ornamented types
& title pages

Nineteenth century
ornamented types
& title pages

Note that in the first example the most logical division has to be abandoned when it would entail an emphasized line beginning with an unimportant word, in this case 'of'.

Similar results can be attained by a change of alphabet. A line of capitals occurring between lines of lowercase, or vice versa, stands out by force of contrast. When change of alphabet is used along with a larger type size to lend emphasis, the effect is particularly happy:

A psychological
study of
TYPOGRAPHY

A PSYCHOLOGICAL
STUDY OF
typography

Nineteenth century
ORNAMENTED TYPES
& title pages

NINETEENTH CENTURY
ornamented types
AND TITLE PAGES

In each instance the emphasized line must still *appear* larger than the others. In the examples on the left, where the emphasized lines are in capitals, they do not have to be in a larger point size than the rest, but in the right-hand examples the lowercase lines must be set several sizes larger in order to appear more important.

Final choice of sizes and alphabets depends on the overall group shape, as encountered in section 4. Of the examples shown here, which are the most satisfactory?

Now continue with the layout. A sticker is a small piece of gummed paper printed with a simple advertising message. Confine your choice to roman and italic, capitals and lowercase of normal weight of a text face. The purpose of this job, however, calls for type sizes as large as possible, but try not to crowd the interlinear space or approach too near to the edges of the paper.

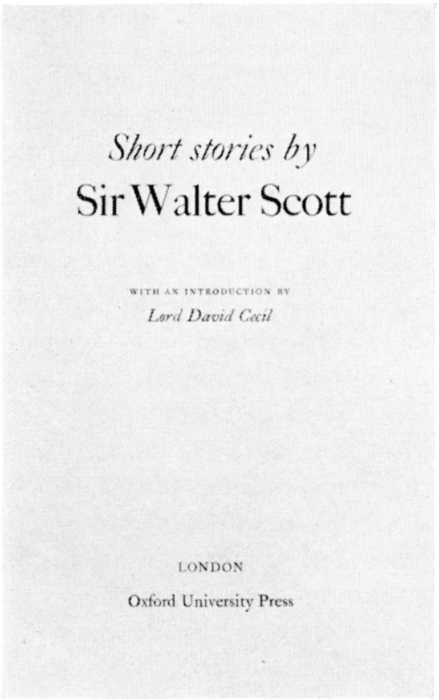

Short stories by
Sir Walter Scott

WITH AN INTRODUCTION BY
Lord David Cecil

LONDON
Oxford University Press

28

So far we have only faced the problems met with in the display of a single phrase, in which all words are virtually of equal importance and space is used only to separate optically words and lines. As soon as the copy becomes more extended, the importance to the reader of its different parts is likely to vary and this must be reflected in the typographic treatment.

It is a principle of learning that information is best presented in groups each group comprising related ideas. The first task of the typographer is to read the copy and sort it out into its logical groupings. The space between groups varies in extent and reflects the closeness or otherwise of the logical connection between them.

Next he estimates the relative importance of each group to the reader and chooses type sizes accordingly. Type below 10pt is hardly readable and should only be specified for matter which is not strictly essential to understanding. Contrary to expectation, perhaps, larger type sizes, say over 24pt, become progressively more difficult to read at normal reading distance, particularly when more than a few words are involved.

The copy here falls logically into three parts, indicated by the oblique strokes. The title is the most important item and must appear so, by its size and also by its position around the focal point of the page. The imprint is of little interest to the reader and can be relegated to the foot of the page and a small type size. The year of publication can be displayed fairly prominently if it is presumed that the pamphlet is kept up to date by being printed every year. All sizes will be conditioned by the fact that the layout is for a title page requiring less strength of treatment than a cover, and always being read at normal reading distance.

In all layouts from now on it will be necessary to indicate type area and margins. The type area is the rectangle inside which all print must appear being surrounded by unprinted margins. The compositor makes up his type page to the full type area, blanking out with spacing material where no type appears.

Margins fulfil a useful as well as an aesthetic purpose, allowing space for handling the sheet without obscuring the print and providing a frame around the text area which concentrates attention on it. The first thing is to decide on the measure (type area width), in 12pt ems and check that it is readily obtainable furniture length. Most common sizes held in stock by printer are:

12 14 15 16 18 20 22 24 25 26 28 30 32 34 35 36 40 42 45 48 50 55 60 ems

Prepare a working layout for the title page of a pamphlet.
Copy: 'Specimens of type faces, ornaments and borders/The College of Art/19xx'. Trimmed page size is 215×125mm (8½×5in).

Intermediate sizes may be available, especially in larger printers. The proportion of measure to paper width depends on the nature and amount of copy, but a good average is around three-quarters of the paper width. Thus a 125mm (5in) paper width might have a measure of 22 or 24 ems, leaving margins of about 4 ems or 3 ems respectively on each side.

Normal practice for a single sheet or a pamphlet with few pages is to observe equal margins left and right. The same space can be allocated to the head margin. The foot margin should always be greater because the eye does not accept mechanical centring of units from top to bottom in an area. An increase of half as much again is often suitable. The depth of the type area is also stated in 12pt ems, though in matters of page depth it is not necessary to keep to furniture lengths.

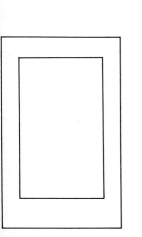

It is a useful aid to positioning type lines to begin with the bottom group, in this case: 'The College of Art'. Again keeping to one weight of a text face, choose a suitable alphabet around minimum readable size. When calculating the width made by type lines in sizes up to 14pt, the method used for large sizes (section 5) becomes tedious and inaccurate. Instead, assume that all letters and spaces are of equal width and count off against the specimen alphabet the number contained in the copy. In the present instance the total number of letters and spaces is 18, which takes us to R in the alphabet. Measure this distance to get the approximate length the line will make when set in this particular alphabet.

When initial capitals are set with lowercase, count each capital as equivalent to two lowercase letters in width, that is, 21 instead of 18 or u in a lowercase alphabet. If level capitals or small capitals are chosen, add a point per character for letterspacing.

Centre this line at the extreme foot of the type area you have drawn on the layout sheet. Do not attempt to trace or draw type sizes up to 14pt, but rule two faint lines the height of the type, mark clearly the line length as calculated, and write in the copy neatly. Make no attempt to letter but show the difference between capitals and lowercase (clearly indicating punctuation, if any) thus:

The College of Art

THE COLLEGE OF ART

As for the title group, decide first on sizes, alphabets and logical, shapely division into lines.

The addition of other matter under the top group requires that the title be lifted to a higher position than if it appeared alone. The more wording that is printed below the main matter, the higher it must go if the correct optical positioning of the group on the page is to be maintained.

29

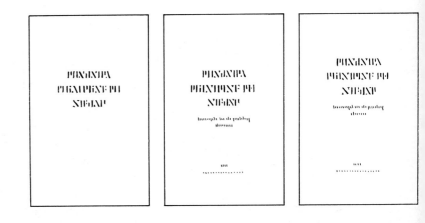

The first illustration shows the employment of the Golden Section in the placing of the title group, as outlined in section 5. The second demonstrates the optical lowering of the title which occurs when other copy is added below it, and the last restores the upper groups to a satisfying position.

The third and last element in the layout consists only of '19xx', which as suggested possibly deserves more prominence than the imprint but much less than the title, and would be well placed between these two groups. It is again important to avoid a position exactly midway between, therefore a decision has to be taken as to whether the date belongs logically to the title or to the imprint.

Complete the layout and mark-up. Finally, examine critically the total shape formed by all the line ends and groups in the job and decide whether improvements can be made.

9 variety within unity

Human nature craves order, so that the mind can understand and relate. If that order is too mechanical and rigid, however, it becomes inhuman and monotonous. The object in typography, as in other design fields, is to establish a logically ordered unity, enlivened with variety of detail.

Prepare a working layout for a cover, finished size 230×100mm (9×4in), incorporating the wording: 'A catalogue of books and magazines on typography available to students of hand composition/College of Printing'.

The paper size in this project is deep and narrow, which affects the design in several ways apart from adding interest by its relative unusualness. To preserve a pleasing location of the type area within the paper size, for example, the foot margin has to be increased in proportion to the other margins as the sheet becomes more elongated. At the same time the focal point tends to occur higher than before in pages of this shape:

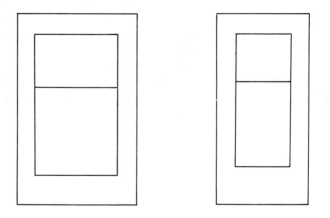

Typeface and alphabet choice are also affected, as is the process of breaking lines. The aim must be to use the additional depth to avoid a crowded appearance at the sides. This can partially be accomplished by splitting the title into more lines, as far as logic permits. We have already noticed that lowercase is more economical in width and occupies more depth than its equivalent in capitals. Also, by choosing a typeface which is narrow in design, such as Times or Ehrhardt, the proportions of type and paper can be harmonized.

The points made in section 7 regarding variation of type size and alphabet within a lengthy title apply with particular force to the present copy. There is a good case for emphasizing 'typography' and diminishing the importance of 'available to students of hand composition', making three distinct levels of emphasis within the title group. Additional space above and below 'typography' helps to subdivide this rather large group into its logical parts, and throws more emphasis on the main word by isolating it further.

For the sake of variety as well as clarity, it is best to specify three distinct alphabets as well as sizes within the group. Compare the following treatments of a similar piece of copy:

32

A guide to
COLOUR
*for the user
of print*

A GUIDE TO
colour
FOR THE USER
OF PRINT

A GUIDE TO
colour
*for the user
of print*

Italic lowercase against a background of roman capitals presents the most striking contrast, but liveliness and interest are created by any alternation of alphabets. A book fount such as we are at present limiting ourselves to has five basic alphabets: ROMAN CAPITALS, SMALL CAPITALS, roman lowercase, *ITALIC CAPITALS* and *italic lowercase*. The first two together offer no contrast and, as italic capitals have already been dismissed as of limited usefulness, only three really contrasting alphabets are available to the student at this stage.

As with division of lines, variation of alphabet must follow the sense of the copy. Never make arbitrary changes not justified by the meaning of the wording, such as

A GUIDE TO COLOUR
for the user of
PRINT

and usually avoid change of alphabet within a line, such as the commonly seen, but unsightly

COLLEGE of ARTS and CRAFTS

Adjacent groups always gain in distinctiveness from being set in different alphabets.

Make a habit from now on of sketching to a reduced scale a number of alternative arrangements for the copy in hand. It helps you to choose, from the various permutations of size, alphabet, line division and spacing, the most satisfactory compromise between the demands of logic, variety and shape. With practice such thumbnail sketches can be accurately done to scale providing a quick method of visualizing the finished layout. For the moment do not attempt to draw these smaller than linear half-size (in this exercise that is 115×50mm).

Design a title page for a booklet, trimmed size 165×215mm (6½×8½in). Copy: 'The classical language of architecture/by John Summerson/ British Broadcasting Corporation/ 19xx/London'. Make a number of miniature roughs and prepare a working layout from the most satisfactory.

The copy is similar to the previous example, but the format is oblong (landscape) instead of upright (portrait). How does this influence the relative foot margin to be allocated and the visual placing of the title group? Is the date important?

Title pages
from an exhibition catalogue
for the National Gallery of Scotland
and a book
by Aberdeen University Press

Old Master
Drawings

FROM THE COLLECTION OF
DR AND MRS FRANCIS SPRINGELL

NATIONAL GALLERY OF SCOTLAND
July to September 1965

*Aberdeen
University Press*

———

AN ACCOUNT OF THE PRESS
FROM ITS FOUNDATION IN 1840
UNTIL ITS OCCUPATION
OF NEW PREMISES
IN 1963

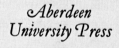

BY

ALEXANDER

KEITH

ABERDEEN
University Press

10 using bold type

In most of the common text faces, more alphabets are available than the five previously listed. **BOLD CAPITALS** and **bold lowercase** bring the total to seven, and in certain founts ***BOLD ITALIC CAPITALS*** and ***bold italic lowercase*** give a maximum of nine alphabets.

Bold type is yet another way of giving emphasis, in addition to those already explored: greater apparent size, contrasting alphabet, isolation and position about the focal point of the page. Bold type is normally used in conjunction with some or all of these. Within text matter, however, bold may be the only possible means of emphasizing a heading.

In display work bold is best confined to main lines. A line set in bold face does not need as large a point size as one of normal weight to have the same importance, a useful fact when space is short. On the other hand, the heavier a type line appears, the more white space should surround it, to throw it into relief.

A guide to

COLOUR

*for the user
of print*

A guide to

COLOUR

*for the user
of print*

Bold types also add to the liveliness of a design. An effect of variety is helpful in arousing interest in the wording and we have already noted several devices which combat monotony: change of alphabet, change of type size (scale) and variety of spacing between groups. The possibility of introducing a much darker element on the page extends the resources for diversity by increasing the tonal contrast between areas of print.

The use of varied sizes of type within a layout has already given some degree of contrast between the heavier look of the big sizes and the lighter appearance of the small. Now bold type in the larger sizes increases this tonal contrast. The effect is best appreciated by half-closing the eyes when looking at a printed page. Text settings and lines in smaller sizes take on a grey texture, while bold, large type shows as a darker patch.

Contrast between areas of tone is effective only if properly handled. In typography the dark areas should be very much in the minority, the result aimed at in a simple layout being an overall white/grey livened with a darker-toned area at the point of maximum emphasis. Bold type throughout a job destroys both variety and emphasis, looks clumsy and frequently lacks legibility. Indeed, the setting of any unimportant line in bold of a small point size can be seen to be a self-contradiction. Occasions when this practice is useful will, nevertheless, arise later.

The intelligent introduction of bold type always increases the visual impact of print. It can be used whenever the nature of the work demands it, on covers and in advertisements, for example, but not often in such jobs as title pages of books or formal invitations.

When preparing thumbnail sketches for this exercise try to give an impression of the tonal values of the various groups and lines. In addition to an HB pencil for lines of average weight and size, use a softer pencil to indicate the darker tones obtained with bolder and larger lines. If desired, use a hard pencil for type in text sizes. In roughs and layout it is only the *relative* tonal values of the type which should be simulated. Make no attempt to match the extreme blackness of printer's ink.

Design a cover, finished size 200×125mm (8×5in), for the following copy: 'A selection of papers and boards for the use of students/ Spicemans Limited/Head office: 19 Old Bridge Street, Manchester M2 1FB'. Use a text face provided with bold in addition to its normal weight.

Cover of *Signature* March 1937
printed black on grey antique laid

SIGNATURE

A QUADRIMESTRIAL
OF TYPOGRAPHY AND GRAPHIC ARTS
EDITED BY OLIVER SIMON

5

MARCH 1937

PUBLISHED AT 108 GREAT RUSSELL STREET, LONDON, W.C.

PRICE: THREE SHILLINGS NET

A number of points of detail arise in connection with the copy. A basic principle of good typography is that no mark should appear on the paper unless justified on the basis of helping the reader to understand the copy. Punctuation should be cut to the minimum and, indeed, we have used none so far. Now the style of the address raises the question for the first time.

The comma after 'Street' can be omitted if it comes at the end of a line, but must be included if it is in the middle. The same is true of the colon, especially if 'Head office' is set in a different alphabet from the address itself. No comma is ever needed before the postal code, nor are points desirable between its characters.

Small capitals are less obtrusive than capitals for the postal code, but their use depends on non-lining figures being available in the fount used: M2 1FB or M2 1FB.

Do not use abbreviations such as 'St' for Street. Such contractions derive from handwriting and almost the only acceptable ones in print are: Mr, Mrs, Dr, & and when unavoidable, Ltd.

Put these principles into practice in all subsequent work. It should not be assumed here, any more than with client's copy, that the capitalization and punctuation given are correct. Some reference books are listed at the end.

Publisher's leaflet
set in Plantin and Plantin bold

SOUTHSIDE » SPES ALTERA VITAE

Fifteen Poems and a Play

BY SYDNEY

GOODSIR

SMITH

» SOUTHSIDE, the new Scottish imprint, will make its *début* by publishing *Fifteen Poems and a Play*, a new book of poetry by SYDNEY GOODSIR SMITH which contains: the text, complete and unabridged, of *The Stick-Up, or Full Circle*, the radio-play in which ROBIN ORR found the *libretto* for his opera *Full Circle*, first presented by Scottish Opera at Perth on 10 April 1968; a poetic comment on Lenin's pronouncement that 'three men make a revolution'; one of the most sensitive sequences of love-poems that the author has ever published; *The Twa Brigs*, a delightfully whimsical mono-logue commissioned by the B.B.C. to celebrate the opening of the Forth Road Bridge by H.M. Queen Elizabeth on 4 September 1964; and, for good measure, three *jeux d'esprit* of a still more broadly popular character. ROBIN ORR contributes a musical setting of 'The Kimmers o' Cougate', one of these ribald pieces.

» *Fifteen Poems and a Play* thus combines the talents of two distinguished Scottish artists with the enterprise of a new Scottish publisher. Printed, in a limited edition, by the Aberdeen University Press, it will appeal not only to poetry-readers, but also to opera-goers, book-collectors, and connoisseurs of typographical design and printing.

The publishers are grateful to Scottish Opera for generous help in distributing this leaflet.

11 choice of typeface

The typeface used has so far been left to the student's own choice, provided that a text type, that is, a face suitable in its smaller sizes for continuous composition, was used. It is now time to examine the matter further.

Practical considerations affect selection of fount. As well as the number of alphabets available and the provision of lining or non-lining figures, the relative width of the design is important. Oblong and wide pages prefer wider typefaces; slightly condensed faces suit narrow upright formats.

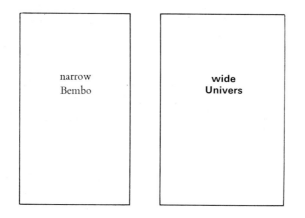

narrow
Bembo

**wide
Univers**

There is also an aesthetic factor. A small range of typefaces may be considered suitable in the interest of maximum legibility. Even within that range, however, a particular fount may express better than another the meaning of a certain piece of copy. Thus Times or Bodoni has a rational, businesslike air, while Bembo or Garamond is altogether more feminine and graceful. Each would be most successful in its proper context, though it is only fair to add that in the hands of an experienced typographer typefaces can be made to take on qualities unsuspected perhaps by their designers.

Reread section 6, dealing with the qualities of capitals, lowercase, roman and italics, in conjunction with this new information. Influence of paper surface on type choice is discussed in section 28.

In the interest of unity, a job should be set in one series throughout, using the alphabets available to obtain contrast, unless positive benefits are to be gained by the introduction of a quite different design of letter. These benefits would normally be more impact on the reader and better visual expression of the copy. The use of a contrasting typeface adds interest to a layout and the parts set in it gain in importance. But the aim must be to secure these advantages without sacrificing the harmony between parts which is essential to good design.

The first rule might therefore be: use together only dissimilar faces. For example, a job set in Baskerville would possibly be improved by having its main lines in Bodoni series, but not by having them in Caslon. There is not enough difference between Caslon and Baskerville for the substitution to look deliberate and meaningful. Bembo and Perpetua are likewise too similar in the same weight to combine happily, but a case could be made for specifying Perpetua bold headings along with Bembo text, since it offers a decisive contrast. The inclusion of Bembo bold in the same layout would confuse the issue, however.

The Economic Facts of Life

—

A series of articles by Harold Wincott reprinted from the
Esso Magazine
(1955/56 issues)

Illustrations by Jennifer Rope

WILSON STEPHENS, Editor of THE FIELD

Greyhounds in the Slips

On nearly one day in three, greyhounds compete in coursing meetings 'under rules' somewhere in the United Kingdom. The rules are those of the National Coursing Club, which is older than the National Hunt Committee and only a little younger than the Jockey Club, the two bodies which control horse racing. Coursing itself, the pursuit of the hare at gaze as opposed to hunting by scent, is

A second rule is that, while the two types chosen must contrast in some way in order to justify the mixture, they must also have some feature in common, to ensure unity of style within the layout. It is easy to select pairs of contrasting typefaces, but it is not so simple to decide when two types are incongruous. Caslon contrasts strongly with Bodoni, but the human irregularities of the one go ill with the geometrical precision of the other. A page of Perpetua looks unpleasant with Baskerville semi-bold display lines, the fine classical sharpness of the former being contradicted by the blunt heartiness of the latter. On the other hand, a setting in Imprint may be enhanced by the use of Ehrhardt semi-bold for the main lines. It is a matter of developed taste, which comes only through repeated contact with type, leading to an understanding of the characteristic personalities of the various designs. Some knowledge of the historical origins of each face is desirable, but is never a firm guide to the selection of a typeface for a particular job, nor does it help much with the problem of combining faces. In the examples reproduced here, Walbaum medium gives a Bembo setting impact and variety, without incongruity of style, while Clarendon combines well with Ehrhardt text.

Typeface should not be changed indiscriminately in the middle of a layout. As with bold type in section 10, the less use made of the contrasting element, the more effective it becomes. Similarly, only main lines are eligible for the added importance given by change of face. The employment of more than two series in a single page is best left until later.

With the added typographic means now at your disposal, prepare another working layout for the exercise given in section 7, improving on impact and liveliness.

39

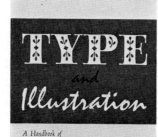

First page of a leaflet
by W. S. Cowell
printed black, red and green
set in Sapphire, Mistral
Bembo and Gill extra bold

Type designs may be divided roughly into two kinds. One is suitable for use in small sizes for continuous setting of text which does not draw attention to itself but combines legibility with a pleasant appearance in the mass. The larger sizes of such faces are quite satisfactory in display work and offer a fair degree of variety and expression. But they are limited in these respects when the copy demands a more forceful treatment.

The other category of type designs is meant to be used only in larger sizes for important lines. The purpose of such display types is to call attention to themselves through their distinctive designs and, while remaining legible, to help express through their shape the meaning of the copy.

A useful exercise in the selection of letter forms to convey meaning is to take words such as those given in the list below and try to letter each in a style which expresses the idea, without exceeding the range of variation permitted to letters which must remain readable. Here are some examples:

Notice that alphabet choice—capitals or lowercase, roman or italics—is still very important. Now attempt these, first inventing appropriate letter forms of your own, then searching in Berry, Johnson, Jaspert: *The encyclopaedia of type faces* for existing typefaces to fit each word:

ELEGANCE	DARK	FUNNY	URGENT
SPEED	HEAVY	FEARFUL	EFFICIENT
BEAUTY	FAT	SAD	CHILDISH
ENERGY	COLD	EXPLOSIVE	ANTIQUE

The principle can be extended to products and services. The skill learned is intended to be applied later to the selection from available types of the most suitable to the work in hand.

PAINT	GLASS	ELECTRONICS	CHURCH
PENS	WATCHES	CHOCOLATE	BANK
CONCRETE	FASHION	PRINT	JAZZ
PERFUME	STEEL	ART	MUSIC HALL
COAL	FLOWERS	RAILWAYS	HOLIDAYS
WINE	BEER	MATHEMATICS	NEWS
SCULPTURE	BOOKS	SCHOOL	ARMY

The availability of display types is an important factor in their use. It is unrealistic to obtain specimen sheets of attractive faces and assume that they are stocked or can easily be obtained by the printer. Every reputable printer has his own type book and as far as possible types should be selected from this.

There are three sources of display types: Monotype, line composition and the type foundries. In the case of line composition it is necessary to keep to what the printer already possesses. With Monotype, display sizes are cast on the premises from hired matrices, but it is not economic to do this for a single job unless it is a very large order. However, lines and founts of display sizes of Monotype faces not stocked by the printer can often be bought at a local typesetting trade house and this is a common and relatively inexpensive

left
Thorowgood italic
with Times

right
Wallau
with Plantin

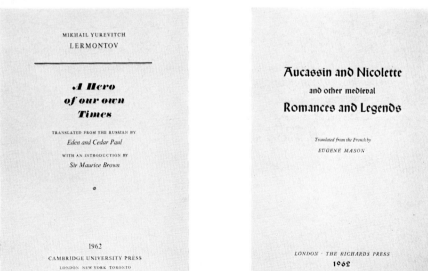

practice. In the case of foundry type the expense of buying in new founts is high, though it is occasionally possible to buy a line only.

To derive full benefit from the capacity of display faces to add emphasis and variety they must be used sparingly, ensuring greatest force of contrast with the accompanying text face, and kept to the largest sizes in a layout. Some display types are not of darker tonal value than the smaller text type they may be wanted to accompany. This is particularly true of open faces, where the strokes of letters are outlined only, and also of certain delicate scripts. Compensate for this by increasing the point size of the display line accordingly.

42

Prepare a caseroom layout for a leaflet printed one side, size 200×125mm (8×5in), incorporating the following wording: 'Midshire Horticultural Society/Annual flower show/19xx/Catalogue 10p'.

Leaflet printed black and brown
for Winston Churchill
Memorial Appeal

14 rules

A range of graded weights of strip rule is available to typographers as a normal resource of the caseroom. In most cases rule is cast on the premises from Monotype matrices and is cut to required lengths by the compositor. The main varieties are shown below with suggested minimum specification, which must be marked up on the layout. As with type in the Monotype system, each face of rule may be cast on several different body widths, such as fine face on 2pt or 2pt full face on 6pt according to the matrices owned by the printer, but this hardly ever concerns the designer outside of table work, which is discussed in section 34. The Monotype serial number, such as 2–R1 for a fine rule on a 2pt body, is sometimes quoted, but because of the large number of very similar rule matrices available this is not recommended unless the designer is quite sure that only this one matrix from the range will suit his purpose and is willing to face the expense of the printer purchasing it and casting rule specially if, as is likely, he does not already possess it.

fine rule (½pt face)	
medium rule (1pt face)	
1½pt full face	
2pt full face	
3pt full face	
4pt full face	
6pt full face	
12pt full face	

18pt and 24pt full face are also in use.

Composite strip rule is stocked by printers to save time in assembly and give a superior join at corners whenever more than a single line is specified. Here is a selection of the most useful:

light and heavy 3pt	
light/heavy/light 6pt	
graded 12pt	

Finally, decorative rules can be asked for, the most useful being the swelled rule, in various lengths, styles and thicknesses. Line composing machines offer a number of these in addition to the ones available from Monotype and, in brass, from typefounders.

There are several advantages to be gained from the use of rules in symmetrical layout, but there is at present a fashionable but unfortunate tendency to use too many in all kinds of print. Optically a straight line, no matter how light, is a powerful visual element on the page and always tends to overpower the type matter along with it and reduce its legibility. Never therefore employ rules unless their presence is justified and care has been taken to avoid undesirable effects.

The most obvious reason for inserting a straight line is to separate one thing from another. A horizontal rule may extend the full width of the measure or even the paper, signifying a total separation of the two pieces of copy so divided. Such a practice may be adopted on a label to separate the printed heading from the space for the filling-in of the addressee.

On the other hand the habit of printing short cut-off rules between groups of lines is no more than a crude duplication of a purpose already adequately served by intelligent use of space, as outlined in section 8, and should normally be resisted. There is however one permissible use of a short horizontal rule and that is to complete a group shape in cases where the copy cannot be broken logically in any way which would produce an acceptable shape. Compare:

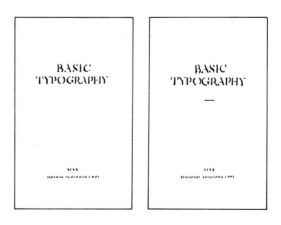

Or a group may require a long line to complete the shape and add width to an impossibly narrow setting. In either case an unobtrusive rule may be the answer, when all else has failed. The cutting-off properties of the rule are always present and its position must still be justified by the sense of the wording, as below:

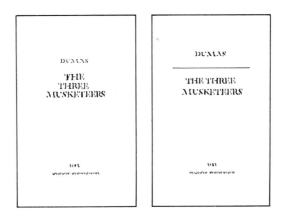

When a single line is used, it should in nearly all instances be fine relative to the size and weight of the type nearby. But a single line has no decorative value and combinations of lines are to be preferred when such an effect is wanted. Care must be taken to select a combination of rules of the correct weight, the thickest similar in width to the main strokes of the typeface in which the main line is set. As for style, types and rules should look as if drawn by the same means. Thus types having contrast between thick and thin strokes suit a combination of heavy and light rules, corresponding to the thicknesses of the strokes in the letter form. Other rules of weights between these extremes can be added if desired.

Walbaum   *Baskerville*   Consort

A further property of rules is that they lend emphasis. The optical effect of a straight line among the complex forms of type characters is to compel the eye to it and sometimes along it. Underlining has long been employed by typists as a means of drawing attention to a word or phrase, but should not be imitated by typographers, who have less crude ways of bestowing importance.

Rules positioned on either side of a main line or group add greatly to its visual impact and are particularly useful when the main copy is brief and tending to be overpowered by such subsidiary matter. The use of two rules in this manner also lends breadth to main lines which are too short for the paper width available, another cause for insignificance. Compare:

46

When positioning type between rules it is important that it should look centred vertically. This is an optical judgement, made first of all by mathematically centring the capital height or x-height of lowercase, then lifting it slightly. Ascenders and descenders on lowercase can be ignored unless they appear to interfere with the impression of equidistance. Spacing between lines must always be less than that between type and rules. In the specimen below the additional space caused by the shorter second line has also had to be taken into account when finding the optically centred position:

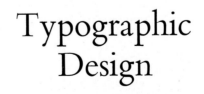

Another visual phenomenon associated with straight lines is the tendency of the eye to be led from the thickest to the thinnest when several are used close together. This fact can be made use of when planning rule combinations by placing the thinnest lines next to the type, to focus attention on it, as shown

CDEFGHIJ **defghij**

The optical result of repeated straight lines is often dazzle, which discourages reading of accompanying wording, even if superficially striking. Occasionally, however, as in the sketch opposite, the product may be eye-catching and forceful while remaining readable:

A case is sometimes made for the inclusion of vertical rules, on the ground that this practice leads the eye down the page. The objections to this are that a strong vertical unit is incongruous and startling in a page composed of type lines which present a uniformly horizontal series, and that our reading habits anyway ensure that the eye will begin top left and proceed to bottom right without such fussy assistance.

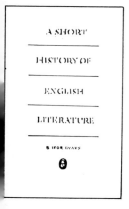

A SHORT

HISTORY OF

ENGLISH

LITERATURE

B IFOR EVANS

Trace the word 'Harmony' several times in different typefaces, weights, sizes and alphabets. Above and below each draw a suitable combination of rules, completing the mark-up.

Title page
*reproduced by permission
of Penguin Books*

MALLARMÉ

INTRODUCED AND EDITED BY
ANTHONY HARTLEY

★

WITH PLAIN
PROSE TRANSLATIONS

PENGUIN BOOKS

15 rule borders

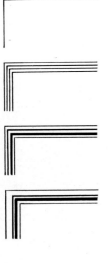

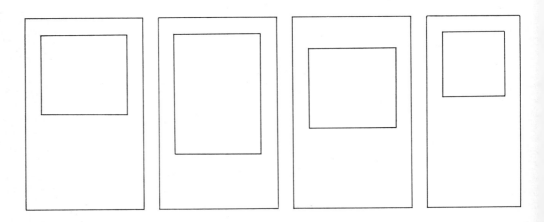

48

Rule surrounding entirely all or some of the type matter on a page can create a highly decorative effect. The design also gains in impact and unity. It is therefore a particularly useful device for handbills, covers and similar work which demand a bold treatment. As the border encroaches on the type area, less space is available for type. This is an advantage when copy is too little for the paper size, but borders should not be used if the result will be to crowd the type matter or oblige specification of point sizes below the ideal.

Rule border, if all round the page, should coincide with the type area, leaving the usual margins. A single rule of any weight is hardly ever satisfactory in this kind of typography, as it has only a bare functional value without decorative appeal. Combinations involving one weight with equal spacing between tend to look monotonous. By using varied thicknesses as outlined in the previous section, interest is created, even more if unequal spacing is adopted. Compare the successive stages opposite.

Similar benefits of increased emphasis and interest can be had by putting a border round only the most important wording, but the shape of the panel thus made must be suitably related to the shape of the paper. Avoid the panel which itself has an unsatisfactory relationship between its long and short sides, making for example, almost a square. The Golden Section ratio can again be quoted as the most suitable. Acceptable proportions have been established in the examples below:

J. E. M. HOARE RARE BOOKS LTD

42 Berkeley Street, London, W.1

CANADIANA

A supplement to the first catalogue of books and manuscripts

The striking optical impression made by straight lines framing an area concentrates attention within it. But type which approaches too closely to the border runs the risk of being overpowered by the rules. Indeed it is advisable, after deciding the margins between border and paper, to determine another type area within the border, following the same pattern: equal margins three sides, extra space at the foot. To ensure good proportions, the space between type and rules should not in the printed job appear equal to the space between the rules and the edge of the paper. Compare these two figures. In the first, space inside and outside the border is uncomfortably similar in extent, but this has been corrected in the second:

Prepare a working layout for a label to be used on a vinegar bottle, printed black on white gummed stock, 75×100mm (3×4in). A decorative rule border is to be incorporated. The copy is: 'Black & Crosswell Limited/ Malt vinegar/Net weight 6 fluid ounces/Manufactured in Great Britain by Black & Crosswell Limited, Birmingham'.

For the first time in these exercises copy is included which is not intended to be read in normal conditions. Type sizes below the minimum required for adequate legibility should be specified for all such parts. Take expected reading distance into account when laying out main lines.

Design the dust jacket for a book, front and spine only, size 255×180mm (10×7in) and 50mm (2in) thick. The copy for the front is: 'The book/ the story of printing and bookbinding/ D.C. McMurtrie'. On the spine the practice is to repeat this wording, but omitting the author's initials and adding at the foot the publisher, in this case, 'Oxford'. Assume that black ink on a buff tinted stock is specified and a rule border is asked for.

Again a strong treatment is called for, taking into consideration the function which a bookjacket fulfils. The spine is of course less forceful, but must closely conform to the cover in style. Where possible, smaller sizes of the same faces and alphabets should be used. The identical rule formation extends to the spine, either in border form or using top and bottom strips only, whichever accommodates better the title within the space available.

In the present exercise the spine is wide enough to allow normal horizontal setting, particularly if the first of the rule arrangements illustrated is adopted. Should a vertical setting be preferred, observe the British Standard recommendation of top-to-bottom reading:

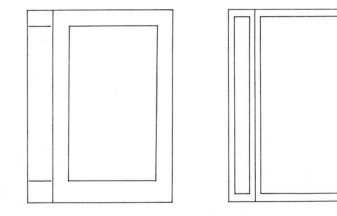

Unit ornaments and unit and strip decorative borders are part of the normal typographic stock of a caseroom. Their use has dramatically declined in recent years owing to the present fashion for 'functional' simplicity in all fields of design. Nevertheless, when working in the traditional idiom typographers cannot afford to ignore the infinite range of decorative and expressive effects obtainable quite economically in this way.

Catalogues of the typefoundries and mechanical composing companies give an idea of the variety of basic units available. The Monotype Corporation in particular offers a wide selection, the majority of which can be used with confidence that the unit itself is well designed. A great aid in the problem of researching in the mass of material is Monotype Recorder, volume XLII,

51

Pages from Nonesuch Press edition of Pindar 1929

PYTHIAN X

Thorax of Larisa in Thessaly, the young King, had this poem written for his friend Hippokleas, who had won the boys' Long Flat Race at Delphi in 498 B.C., and perhaps another event as well.

Hippokleas was the son of a noble family in Pelinna, a town not far from Larisa: but Thorax and his brothers, of the great house of the Aleuadai, were the rulers of all Thessaly. Herodotus calls them *Basilees*, Kings: but Thorax, the eldest, must have borne the title of *Tagos* (first borne by his ancestor, Aleuas the Red), High King perhaps, or rather, since Thessaly was smaller than Ulster, Grand Duke. Anyway he was important and powerful, and the opening words of this poem suggest that he had recently concluded an alliance on equal terms with King Kleomenes of Lakedaimon, and thus ranged himself in the great federation of Hellenes which was preparing to meet the Persians. About eight years later, in 490 B.C.,

· 4 ·

Kleomenes was in trouble at home, and looked to Thessaly for help, but found none. It may well be that Thorax himself depended for his position on Kleomenes' support; for whatever reason and at whatever date—it was well before 480—his position became untenable, and this time he turned to Persia and joined those exiles who hoped that Xerxes would restore them to their honours.

This move was fatal to his own fortunes and to his country's: it was the end of Thessalian importance in Hellas. Of Thorax we know no more. Some of his family, if not himself, patched up an agreement with Sparta and kept some of their honours, and a descendant, Aristippos, was a friend of Sokrates at the end of the century. But after Thorax the Grand-Dukedom passed from the Aleuadai to other families in the southern city of Pharsalos.

The luck of Hippokleas held, as Pindar prayed: he won at Olympia in 492 and 488. By then he was over twenty-five, and a runner's prime is brief.

Pindar was twenty years old when he wrote this, his earliest extant poem. Written for a boy by almost a boy, to be sung at a great feast, it is very gay and happy. Pindar allows,

· 5 ·

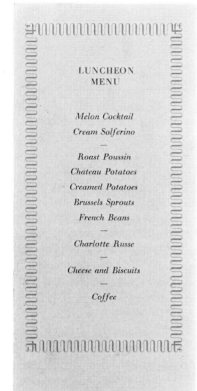

LUNCHEON
MENU

Melon Cocktail
Cream Solferino
—
Roast Poussin
Chateau Potatoes
Creamed Potatoes
Brussels Sprouts
French Beans
—
Charlotte Russe
—
Cheese and Biscuits
—
Coffee

Menu printed red and black

Prepare a working layout for a booklet cover, printed black on light tinted stock, trimmed size 230×150mm (9×6in). The copy is: 'A grammar of type ornament/An analysis and classification of typographic border designs and their behaviour in use/ Part one/Analysis and classification'. A decorative border must be included.

number 1, Spring 1960. Five broadsheets showing a selection of units in various combinations can also be purchased from the Corporation. A study of these provides a grounding for the tasteful and inventive use of decoration wherever copy permits it. The remarks passed in section 13 about local availablity of type apply equally to the specification of ornaments and decorative borders.

Decorative units in strip form are as economic in use as rules and can be mitred or butted at the corners, but attention should be paid to the length of the repeat unit on each of them, because it often dictates the length to which a strip can be cut.

In the same way the body on which a unit ornament is cast determines the length of side of any border made up from it. These are not always in 12pt ems. Often corner pieces are provided whose use is optional. Elaborate decorative set-pieces which entail the assembly of large numbers of separate characters will be costly to set.

As with rules, the style and tonal value of ornaments must be harmonized with those of the types alongside them. Such harmony is not easy to achieve. Only experience and a cultivated sensitivity will bring complete success in this tricky field.

Where access to caseroom facilities exists, an excellent method of approach is to experiment by dabbing border units on an inked roller and stamping them by hand on a sheet of paper. In this way an accurate idea of the total effect of different combinations in the mass can be arrived at.

Occasionally a single ornament or group of ornaments is used, for much the same purpose as the small cut-off rule (see section 14) but with greater decorative result. As with the rule, this must be a rare practice, confined to those cases when the sense of the copy justifies it. The fault most to be avoided in such instances is the choice of an ornament too conspicuous for its wholly subsidiary function. See the illustration on page 33 for a good example.

When making a working layout there is no need to draw in the whole of the decorative border. Trace carefully the units around one corner only and state the manufacturer, serial number and point size of each in the mark-up. Rules may also be added as part of the border if wished.

There are three important ways in which the extra expense involved in colour printing can be justified. In the first place, colour is an instant method of identification. A number of related forms of the same size can be quickly sorted out from each other if a different colour has been used for each. A column of figures demanding special attention is automatically singled out by printing in colour. The practical advantages of colour used in this way should be kept in mind, as many cases will occur when a job so treated would have its handiness improved. Because of colour vision deficiencies in some people, however, colour should never be the *only* method of making important differentiations.

Secondly, colour can be a powerfully attractive visual element which is of great value in those jobs where the reader's attention has to be drawn to the print in the first place, as in most advertising. In all work where colour is included, the brightest colour should be placed at the point where most impact is wanted.

Finally, colour constitutes an expressive language which can often be employed to reinforce the meaning of the copy, particularly where mood and atmosphere are to be evoked. This aspect has already been touched on in the opening section.

The cheapest way of introducing colour is to specify tinted stock, provided it is appropriate and feasible in the circumstances. Reference to a paper-maker's or paper merchant's specimens will give an idea of the variety available. Also inexpensive, incurring only a small extra charge over printing in black, is the substitution for black of a coloured ink. In either case certain optical factors arise which deserve discussion.

A black image on a white ground offers an extreme tonal contrast and ensures a high degree of visibility. When a colour replaces white, contrast between print and paper is reduced, necessitating a more emphatic treatment of the type to correct it. This weakening effect is clearly evident in the illustration at the beginning of this section, where an olive was used in place of black. Type should be made larger, bolder or both, depending on the degree of contrast lost. Thus if a yellow or other light tinted stock is used, very little if any increase in size or weight is called for. Indeed, for continuous reading it is generally agreed that a slightly off-white background reduces eye-strain.

Association of Teachers of Printing and Allied Subjects

65 ATPAS CONFER ENCE

Annual National Conference
Glasgow 23-25 April

Cover of a folder
printed in olive on white

visibility   **visibility**   visibility

54

But if a colour of darker value is chosen for the paper, then considerable added strength has to be given to the type to ensure legibility and the right amount of emphasis. Dark colours such as violet are usually impractical, because the degree of enlargement or emboldenment required to make type fully visible itself interferes with legibility. On occasion, however, as in the illustration on this page, the effect can be used to advantage by a proficient designer.

Coloured inks on white paper encounter similar difficulties. The substitution of any colour for black results in a reduction of tonal contrast between print and paper, again dictating stronger treatment of type matter. Here the darkest tones offer the best alternatives to black. Mid-tones such as the hues of green and red demand considerable reinforcement of the type, while their tints and also colours of light value such as yellow or orange may reduce type to illegibility. Those colours which have a red content seem to have a strength greater than their actual tonal value.

Summing up, it can be said that the tonal value of a colour, that is, its lightness or darkness, is the most important single factor in its use in print.

Redesign the exercise completed in section 13, this time assuming that green ink is to be used instead of black. Draw the working layout in the usual way, using an ordinary pencil, but include a sample of the exact colour of green selected. If setting and proofing in this colour are not possible, make a finished drawing as like the printed result as can be, in poster colour on smooth white cartridge paper. This will allow you to make an estimate of the readability of your design.

Part of an exhibition announcement
by Lund Humphries
printed black on violet

18 **a second colour**

Type matter is often printed in two or more colours. As this entails a separate make-up, imposition and printing for each colour, caseroom and machining costs rise steeply. The commonest combination is black with an additional colour.

As colour attracts attention to itself, it is logical that it should be used for important parts of the copy only. Liberal spotting of the colour throughout the layout defeats its own purpose. As with display type and bold faces, maximum effect is gained only by the least possible employment of colour.

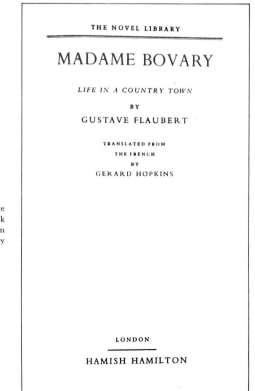

Title page printed red and black for Hamish Hamilton Novel Library

Prepare a working layout for an invitation card, size to fit a 114× 162mm (4½× 6⅜in) envelope, printed black and one colour. The copy is: 'The Trustees of the Wallace Gallery invite you to an exhibition of Dutch seascapes of the seventeenth century, in the Wallace Gallery, Central Square, from Saturday 18th October to Saturday, November 22nd, from 10 a.m. to 6 p.m. daily. Private view: Friday 17 October at 7'.

Several points about this copy require discussion. The principle of minimum punctuation always holds good: punctuation should be omitted where it occurs at the end of a line. Additionally, the form of the dates in the copy is inconsistent. Adopt one form throughout: '25 December 19xx' is the shortest and most businesslike, but '25th' is sometimes preferable in formal work such as that under consideration. The form of a.m. and p.m. is also inconsistent in the copy and needs standardizing.

There is a case for the omission of superfluous words such as 'in the', 'on' and 'from', especially if the shorter lines so made improve the appearance of the card. The word 'seventeenth' is better spelt out, though '17th' can be used should the layout demand it. Initial capitals once more are to be kept to a minimum, but considering the traditional flavour of the subject, rather more than are contained in the copy would seem appropriate.

A careful reading of the wording shows that it consists of one continuous sentence out of which the major line has to be selected, the relative importance of the remaining phrases being reflected in the point size allotted to each. Purely informative matter such as details of place and time should be set plainly, as in continuous text, in a readable size and without meaningless and distracting alphabet changes from one line to the next.

The final sentence in the copy forms a distinct element of its own, to be separated from the rest by a generous space. In practice it is often wise to position this line first, on the extreme foot margin, and then to place the main group visually in the remaining space. This last line may if wished be placed on the extreme left of the type area instead of being centred on the measure. The opposite corner is thus left free for holding the card between finger and thumb.

In an area as small as this card, taking into account also its likely oblong shape, the optical considerations which determined an increase in the foot margin hardly apply and margins can be made equal all round. They should also be fairly narrow.

A coloured pencil will do to draw on the working layout lines intended to print in colour. Specification to the printer of the exact colour wished is discussed fully in section 21 and can be deferred meantime.

ERIC
GILL

When the two colours chosen do not include black, certain fresh problems are posed. These are minimized if a colour of dark value is simply substituted for black in the printing of those parts normally reserved for that ink. A brighter colour would again be prescribed for main lines.

Choice of colours, while influenced by considerations such as have been mentioned and by others still to be met with, is in the last resort an important expressive medium in design. Hues have quite different psychological meanings which must be recognised when making choices. For example, the emotional associations of red include heat, danger, excitement, aggression. Blue may suggest distance, cold and cleanliness. Green evokes peace, quiet and freshness. Red seems to advance out of the page towards the eye. Blue appears to recede. These psychological attributes are outlined simply in Taylor: *Colour Technology*. The point to grasp is that colour is capable of being used to help convey mood or atmosphere, and create a generalized feeling proper to the copy.

The use of a second printing means incidentally that the limitations on the nearness of any two pieces of type are removed, provided that they are in separate printing formes. Thus types can be printed close, touching or overlapping and a number of lively effects can be produced in this way. The device is limited in application, being in fact too striking for most work, but should be kept in mind for the proper occasion. The examples here also present problems of register to the printer:

Prepare a working layout for a book jacket, trimmed size 200×125mm (8×5in) plus a 20mm spine, for an edition of 'Restaurant French for hoteliers, restaurateurs and catering students/Steve Combes/A Practical Press Book'. Use two colours, avoiding black.

58

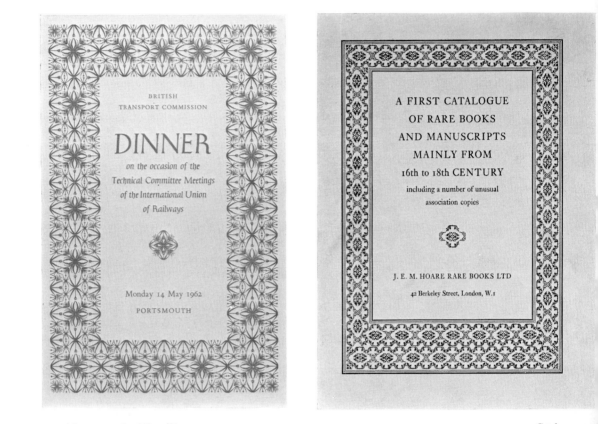

Menu cover printed blue and grey
for British Transport Commission

Catalogue cover
printed red and black on buf
for Hoare Rare Book

20 decorative colour

The printing in colour of rules and ornaments, which are essentially decorative elements in a design, obviously adds to their appeal. As with type, they have to be given a bolder treatment relative to the lightness or darkness of the colour selected. It cannot be too often stressed that the brighter colour should be less extensively used than the basic colour, whether black or its substitute. If the decorative rules or ornaments, when entirely printed in the brighter colour, begin to equal or dominate the rest, it is advisable to put a part of them in the basic colour, as in the diagrams under:

Prepare a working layout for a catalogue cover, size 250×185mm (9¾×7¼in), to be printed in two workings on white board, the copy being: 'A first catalogue of rare books and manuscripts from the 16th to 19th centuries, including a number of unusual association copies/J.E.M. Horne Rare Books Limited/41 Leicester Street, London W1P 6HB'. A decorative border is to be incorporated.

Revise sections 14 to 16 before attempting this exercise.

21 ink specification

Coloured inks are best used straight from the tin, avoiding difficulties o
mixing and matching, but the printer must first be consulted on suitability o
ink to paper. Ink manufacturers supply colour charts which are indispensable
the maker's name and serial number of the ink being added to the mark-u
instructions on the layout. To be on the safe side it is also advisable to enclos
the inkmaker's sample of the printed colour. In spite of these precautions th
apparent colour of the printed job may differ from that expected to a surpris
ing degree. What are the main causes of this?

Smoothness or otherwise of the paper has a great effect on the value of
colour. An ink looks lighter when printed on a very smooth surface but darken
progressively with increasing roughness of paper, owing in part to the manne
in which light is reflected back to the eye. Samples are usually on smoot
stock and therefore unexpected darkening is the more common complaint.

Thickness of ink film also affects value, because with less ink on the surfac
more white paper shines through. Ink film thickness depends on the proces
(see section 49), the stock and the nature of the work. In general, roughe
papers need more ink and formes with heavy solids or illustrations als
demand heavier inking.

Optical illusions alter the apparent tones and hues of colours. These ar
explained in any book on colour theory, including Taylor: *Colour Technolog*
but may briefly be touched on here. The proportion of white paper to in
image affects the apparent colour of the image by force of contrast. That is,
coloured ink used to print a line of small type looks darker than the same in
when overprinting a large area. If small type lines are printed in very dar
colours they tend to look as if printed in black with insufficient density. Whe
black is introduced alongside the colour, however, the colour appears lighte
and brighter by the same force of contrast.

The juxtaposition of any colour with another alters the apparent hue an
value of both, but particularly the one having the smaller area. It tends to tak
on the opposite characteristics of the dominant colour, becoming lighter if th
other is dark and shifting its hue towards the complementary of the other.

Viewing conditions, particularly the nature of the light source, also hav
their influence on the colour seen.

From this brief summary, it should now be appreciated that an elementar
knowledge of the theory of colour is indispensable to the designer for print.

Colours not available from an inkmaker can be mixed to order by th
printer, matching a poster colour patch supplied by the designer. Printer
inks are different in substance from poster colours, and printing paper surfac

differ from drawing paper, so a perfect match cannot be expected.

The simplest kind of mixed colour, and the most frequently prepared, is a tint of a standard ink. There are two ways of obtaining a tint, one by adding opaque white (as the designer does with poster colour or gouache), which results in a fairly opaque ink covering the paper grain and seeming to lie on the surface of the paper, with a rather matt effect. The alternative is to reduce the pigment ratio by adding more vehicle (as when water is added to water-colour), giving a more transparent film which reveals the paper texture and seems an integral part of it. Always specify transparent or opaque when ordering a tint.

When a coloured ink is printed on a coloured stock it often undergoes a change of hue. In letterpress and lithographic inks only black is tolerably opaque (although opaque tints are relatively so) and a translucent ink film allows the underlying colour to show through to a greater or lesser extent. Reference to textbooks on colour will help the student avoid the more calamitous results of this fact and suggest ways of using such colour changes to advantage. But the forecasting of probable colour from overprinting remains difficult even when experimental proofing facilities are to hand. Note that the translucency of printing inks means that it is hardly possible to print light inks on dark stock with satisfactory results. The thicker film of ink which is used with rougher papers helps to reduce translucency, however.

Another important characteristic of an ink, affecting the depth of colour, is its degree of gloss. Tints with white added tend to look matt, otherwise most inks possess a fair sparkle and some are high-gloss. Paper surface is a decisive factor in the amount of gloss which an ink will have when printed, coated stock alone permitting high-gloss affects and rough textures rendering all inks more or less matt. Varnishing or laminating involves additional processing, but gives a higher gloss than is possible from ink alone. Paper surface again affects the result.

On the subject of ink specification, the examples in *The print user's guide to colour* are of considerable interest.

med with one or more ink anufacturers' sample books, select itable inks for each of the exercises mpleted from section 17 to date. rite a full specification on the yout in every case. If a colour has be mixed, provide a poster colour tch. Detail whether translucent or aque, gloss or matt, where propriate.

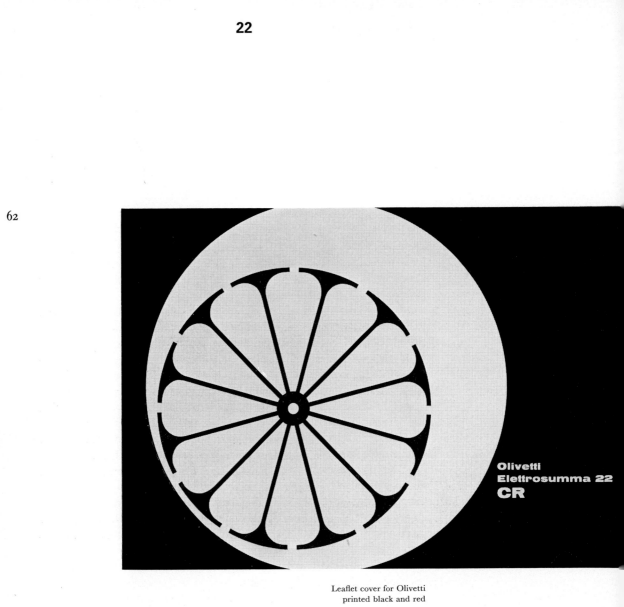

Leaflet cover for Olivetti
printed black and red

22 asymmetric design

In working out the exercises so far, you will have found that the central placing 63
of all type lines achieves perfectly satisfying results. But in modern times, for
a number of reasons, layouts composed on quite different principles have been
increasingly preferred. The first experiments in off-centre placings were made
towards the end of the last century at a time when novelty of type design had
reached absurdity and could do no more to create visual interest in print
which, because of mass production, had lost the status which attaches to rarity
and expensiveness. Advertising, too, was beginning to demand a more
insistent style than the symmetrical, based as it is on book design. The present
preoccupation with the disposition of type on the page is only an intensifica-
tion of these historical tendencies.

It was not until the 1920s, however, that a systematic theory and practice of
design were evolved, in and around the Bauhaus, the great pioneering school
of the modern style. Founded on the ideas and achievements of abstract art,
the New Typography has served ever since as a framework of reference for all
typographic design which tries to reflect twentieth-century life and thought.
One main distinguishing feature of this style, as opposed to traditional design,
is its asymmetry.

In the opening chapter of Lewis: *Typography: basic principles* the author
sketches briefly the historical influences on the visual language in use today
and shows typical specimens of print from the development period. Gropius's
own account of the new ideas in design has been reprinted: *The new architecture and the Bauhaus*. In Rowland: *The shapes we need* the nature of this visual
language in all fields of design is further traced and described. The other books
by Rowland, comprising a simple but sound guide to the basic concepts of
good contemporary design, are listed in the bibliography and strongly
recommended.

64

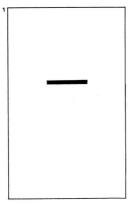

When a type line is positioned centrally on a page, the effect aimed at is that of fig. 1, with the implication of a central vertical axis and the line itself positioned in an optically pleasing relationship to top and bottom of the sheet. The ratio suggested was about 2:3.

If a similarly satisfying position is now to be reached with the line off-centre, this useful ratio may be applied across the page as well as vertically. In the subsequent figures the ratio 2:3 can be recognized when the spaces to left and right of the type are compared, as well as the spaces above and below. Note that a low position, with the ratio reversed as in figs. 3 and 5, is perfectly acceptable in asymmetric design:

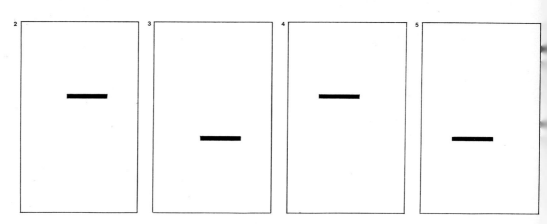

Proof or trace the word 'specimens' in 36pt lowercase and use the ratio to position it on a sheet of card 200×130mm or 8×5¼in in each of the four possible situations. Compare the visual effect of asymmetric placings compared with the symmetric one. Do you agree that with this extended use of the ratio the sense of order and good proportion has been retained, with the benefit of added visual interest, especially in the case of low positions?

The shape of the paper is also subject to the rules of good proportion. The most satisfying of all rectangles is achieved when the sides are in this same relationship of 2:3, as in the above figures. Rectangles departing from this shape lose those often desirable qualities of order and correctness. The square by comparison is dull and less capable of interesting division internally. Worst of all are those rectangles with one pair of sides slightly longer than the other. The eye can only be irritated by such indecisiveness. If the line of type in the above exercise were much longer, there would be little perceptible difference between the spaces on either side of it when the ratio was applied. The line would look as if badly centred, and the general affect would be displeasing.

On the other hand, rectangles which increase the ratio between side lengths, while failing in the power of giving quiet satisfaction, gain in the possession of dramatic tension, which intensifies as the proportion becomes more extreme. This can be appreciated from a study of the figures below:

In a similar manner the capacity of a type arrangement to convey a sense of urgency can be fully realised only if the 2:3 ratio is abandoned. The greater degrees of tension arising from the use of more extreme ratios can be seen in figs. 6 to 10:

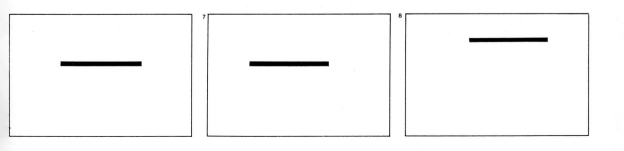

Fig. 6 once more demonstrates the feeling of rest which is experienced with symmetry and fig. 7 uses the 2:3 ratio in both directions. In the remaining figures the type placing can be felt to become increasingly dramatic as the ratios, vertically and laterally, are made more extreme.

Much of the impression of urgency which such layouts produce derives from an illusion which is present in two-dimensional design, that of movement. In fig. 6 the type is static but in fig. 7 a perceptible drift of the line towards the left can just be detected. In fig. 8 there is also a floating move-

Letterheading
printed black, brown and grey
for Plunket McNair

ment, in fig. 9 the drift is definite and to the right, and in the final figure maximum impact is secured when the type actually collides with the edge of the page—not of course a recommended practice!

The explanation of how this important optical illusion arises may be that when the eye falls on a page it naturally focuses first on the area occupied by the type in fig. 6. If, as in the subsequent figures, the line is not encountered within that area, the eye must move to find it, causing a sensation of movement which is greater the further the eye has to travel.

Movement in our everyday experience supposes a force which does the moving and indeed we get the impression of a pull exerted between the edge of the paper and the nearest part of the type line, which becomes more pronounced as the type approaches the edge and reaches a peak of tension when the two touch. Now repeat the exercise carried out earlier, trying to feel the tension as the line is placed nearer the edge of the sheet.

It may be remarked that it is easier to detect apparent movement towards the right, as in figs. 8 to 10, than to the left, as in fig. 7. This is consistent with the theory above, as reading involves eye movement from left to right which reinforces a motion in the same direction but conflicts with one in the opposite direction. In practice this means that asymmetric placings to the right are generally more satisfactory than similar placings to the left of a page.

Another factor which enhances the dramatic effect is the influence of the white space. The habit of left-to-right reading ensures that the eye enters the page top left. Should it meet its object, the wording, immediately, there is no incentive for it to wander further and a reduced awareness of the total page and its proportions must follow. If, on the contrary, the eye encounters only space at first, the delayed entry of the wording contributes to the dramatic effect. Examine figs. 3 and 9, comparing their use of white space with that in other figures. Again the conclusion is that type positioned to the right has important advantages, and lines in low placings have more dramatic effect.

To sum up, asymmetric layout is subject to the factors of movement, tension and space. These must be appreciated and taken into account when planning the design. Exactly how this is to be carried out in practice has still to be discussed.

STD1STD1
STD1STD1

Final call for entries- STD1 Exhibition

CALL FOR ENTRIES: Members of the STD are invited to submit 5 specimens of advertising or print material with typography or letter form in the predominating element
DEADLINE: Friday 15th April 1966 Entries to be sent to STD Exhibition, Image Design, 6 Ludgate Square, London EC4

All entries to contain name and address of designer. This information to be attached to back of each entry

Exhibition announcement
printed red and black
for the Society
of Typographic Designers

Cover a large sheet of paper with rectangles of varying proportions, both oblong and upright. Compare them and tick off those which have satisfying proportions. In each of those place a word or short line in an asymmetric position, different in each case. Again compare and evaluate.

68

All that has already been learned about logical grouping and spacing, choice of type size and alphabets, variety and use of colour equally applies here. The new problem is how to relate all the type matter on the page to the main line whose positioning was studied in the last section. In traditional display all lines are centred on an imaginary axis running down the middle of the page. In asymmetry, this axis no longer exists and further copy must relate to a vertical axis whose location has yet to be decided.

In section 4 the ability of the eye to complete shapes which are only suggested to it was remarked upon as being the basis of form in typography. It was pointed out then that the predominant visual impression of a line of type is two horizontal parallel lines. (If we care to distinguish further, we notice that the lower line is of slightly greater importance.) It was also recognized at the same time that the beginning and end of a type line are seen as vertical marks which are capable of extension. The line beginning is under-standably more important than the end. Other minor verticals are suggested by the beginnings of each main word in the line. None of these is particularly noticeable, however, until brought to the attention by some method of reinforcement.

National Graphical Association

National Graphical Association

If the remaining type matter in the copy is lined up under or over any one of these verticals, the illusion of a straight vertical line is created so strongly that it becomes a dominant feature on the page and can be utilized as the vertical axis:

National Graphical Association

National Graphical Association

National Graphical Association

The proportions implied by the intersecting horizontal and vertical axes are important, since they are the most obvious divisions of the paper area. All that has been said about the use of ratios to place a line of type asymmetrically on a page must be applied to the placing of the vertical and horizontal axes formed when several type lines are involved. The choice of positions will of course be limited by the nature and amount of copy.

In these examples the way in which rectangles are formed by the crossing of the axes is clearly visible. In fig. 1 their proportions are particularly happy, the 2:3 ratio applying to paper size, the placing of both axes and two of the interior rectangles, one of the remaining rectangles being a square. The intersection of the axes lies on the diagonal in this arrangement.

In fig. 2 only the vertical axis observes the 2:3 ratio, the length of the main line having demanded its positioning to the left, just as the amount of copy preceding the main line has dictated a low placing for the horizontal axis. More extreme proportions are seen in fig. 3, with, as expected, a heightening of dramatic effect. Note the square again, top right.

The degree of visual interest in the shape of a design is another concern in its organization. The four diagrams demonstrating the creation of a vertical axis can be simply represented thus:

The two forms where a cross is made are more stable and interesting than the other pair. Most asymmetric layouts are constructed about the cross, the strongest of all elementary shapes.

To sum up the content of this vital section, it can be said that the basic human need for formal unity can be satisfied in asymmetric typography by forming a vertical and horizontal axis to which all type lines will conform. The success in formal terms of the resulting layout depends greatly on the proportions and degree of visual interest present.

70 On a sheet of paper draw a number of pleasing rectangles of different shapes, both oblong and upright. Divide each by a vertical and horizontal line to produce a satisfactory relationship between the spaces on either side of the lines, and to make well-proportioned rectangles in each case. Then indicate by drawing in a manner similar to that in figs. 1 to 3 possible placings of type matter.

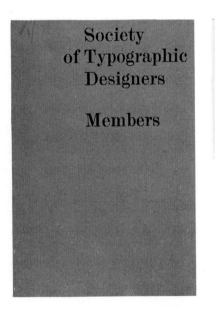

Society
of Typographic
Designers

Members

Booklet cover
for the Society
of Typographic Designers
printed black on dark green

Lund Humphries letterheading
printed black and blue

To understand the foregoing principles it is essential to apply them in practical
exercises, simple to begin with.   71

Design a booklet cover, 150×230mm
(6×9in), copy: 'College of Art/
Specimens of type faces/available to
students of the printing and graphic
design departments/November 19xx'.
Use a text face with seven or nine
alphabets.

Margins are still of use in this style of layout, but should be kept to a minimum, even when the copy consists of only a few words, and little or no
increase made to the foot margin. It is possible that no type will touch any of
the extremities of the type area, especially to top and left, but foot and right-
hand margins can be helpful in making the disposition of type fit comfortably
paper size and shape.

First repeat the exercise of choosing and tracing a suitable type and size
for the main line 'Specimens of type faces', and of finding an optically acceptable position for it on the page according to the principles learned in section
23. With the main line provisionally placed, select a vertical axis which
accords with the ideas put forward in section 24. Is there enough space left
to accommodate the rest of the copy without crowding or illogical positioning
on the page? If not, begin again by trying the main line elsewhere. When all
three conditions have been successfully complied with, trace the main line
onto the finished layout and lightly indicate the two axes.

The long line of secondary copy which must logically follow closely after
the title needs breaking into several shorter lines, following the normal rules.
Never attempt to justify such lines in the mistaken belief that the appearance
will somehow be tidier if the lines line up at the right as well as the left. The
rigid framework of horizontal and vertical needs somewhere the relief of
curved, non-geometric shapes. Unjustified lines provide this. The shape
suggested by the right-hand edge of such groups should receive the same
attention as was paid to the shapes of symmetric groups in section 4, and
should follow similar principles:

While this subsidiary group must follow immediately the main line, since they
are part of the same sentence, the two remaining items in the copy are quite
independent and should be treated accordingly. 'College of Art' has the sense

of a heading and asks to be put to the left or at the top, where it will precede the title. The date would more suitably be printed at the foot, possibly towards the right.

With the aid of miniature roughs the student should be able to fix each in a situation which is also visually pleasing, while relating to one or other of the axes in the way recommended.

The success of any printed job depends primarily on the extent to which the wording has been logically presented to the reader. It is the typographer's business to 'digest' the copy and use all the means at his disposal—typefaces, sizes, spacing and positioning on the page—to 'explain' the sense of the copy, deciding for the reader in advance questions of sequence and relative importance. The eye should be given a beginning and an end, remembering the convention of left-to-right and top-to-bottom reading. All of the copy should be capable of being read without awkward jumps of the eye, such as unnatural right-to-left and upward directions. Criticisms on those grounds can be made against all of the following layouts:

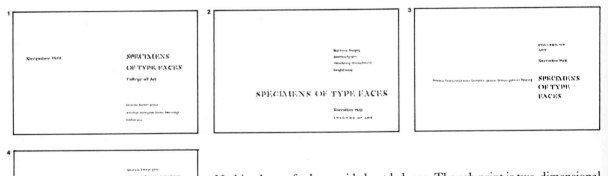

Nothing has so far been said about balance. Though print is two-dimensional, our vision is so accustomed to the real world that we interpret it in terms of that world. The paper becomes space and images printed on the paper occupy positions in space. They also appear to have mass, seeming heavier or lighter in proportion to their area and density. If these masses do not appear to be held in equilibrium on the page, the design must be unsatisfactory.

In the real world equilibrium is achieved when the forces acting on masses are equal. In symmetric layout, as discovered, all lines are in a state of rest, though they must still contend with the force of gravity. But as the mass of type is evenly distributed on either side of an imaginary central vertical axis, there is no danger of it appearing to fall over to the left or right.

With asymmetric layout, on the other hand, the vertical axis is not central and equal distribution of type masses on either side of it will not produce a balanced result. In fact the vertical axis acts in a similar manner to a fulcrum, so that a small mass distant from the axis balances a larger mass nearer to the axis. This is evident in fig. 3, where owing to the extreme placing of the vertical axis a large mass is needed on the right to balance the very small mass on the left. Gravity, however, is not the only force at work in asymmetry, as has been seen in section 23, and the resolution of the tensions created in such designs can only be accomplished intuitively by the practised eye. In fig. 4 an equilibrium has failed to be established.

The student at this point is advised to read Sausmarez: *Basic design*, with special reference to chapters 3 and 4, for a deeper understanding of this part of the subject. Then do the exercise.

The spacing between groups, though in the first place a reflection of the logical connection between their wordings, also makes optical divisions of the page area. A final check should be made on the layout, comparing proportionally the spaces between groups, to ensure that a satisfying set of relationships exists. This can be more easily seen if the layout is turned on its side. The figure below, derived from the illustration, shows that an interestingly varied set of spaces has been established in this design.

Invitation
printed black and violet
on cream card

DESIGN
IN
PRINT
1962

An exhibition produced by the British Federation of
Master Printers in collaboration with the Council of Industrial Design
will be shown at Stow College of Printing, 121 Cowcaddens Street,
Glasgow C2, at the dates and times which are shown overleaf.
The exhibition is intended to be seen rather by printers and their
employees than by customers.

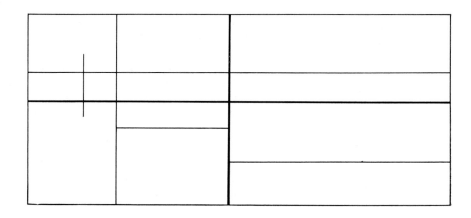

Publisher's leaflet by Studio Vista
printed black and red on white

Announcing a new practical series for today's artist, art student and teacher

Studio paperbacks

are introductory handbooks to various fields of art and design.
Original in approach and attractive to look at they explore their
subjects fully through a wide variety of illustrations (many in
colour) and a clear, authoritative text. The authors – all well-
known artists and designers – are concerned to establish the
basic principles behind the problems confronting a practitioner:
they write forcefully and lucidly, with a marked lack of jargon.
The series, edited by John Lewis FSIA, for the last twelve years
a tutor in graphic design at the Royal College of Art, should
prove of particular value to students taking the new Diploma in
Art and Design.
The first four volumes (paperback 10s 6d, hardback 21s each)

Unesco Publications

scientific and technical

Scientific and Technical

UNESCO booklet cover
printed black and orange-brown
on white

26 sanserif types

Originally sanserif (grotesque) was introduced in the early nineteenth century as a high-impact novelty type for advertising purposes. It remained a display face of limited application until the 1920s, when the New Typographers singled it out as the letterform which best embodied their design ideals. The sanserifs produced in this period are geometric, rational and anonymous, reflecting the technological and democratic aspects of the modern age and these qualities remain in the present fashionable neo-grotesques, more human and subtle though these are.

The New Typographers wished sanserif to replace entirely roman types, with their renaissance background. Today this extreme view is as yet held only by a minority of designers, among them Müller-Brockmann in his book *The graphic artist and his design problem*, but sanserifs are increasingly in evidence in all classes of print save books. Most typographers consider roman type more legible for continuous reading (though recent experimental work by Zachrisson has not supported this contention) and are unwilling to forego the immense expressive range of the serifed display faces.

Current practice is to choose sanserif whenever the copy demands it, particularly when an impression of modernity is wanted. But sanserif cannot be employed according to the practices proper to roman, any more than its characters can share the proportional basis of roman. Especially, sanserif is difficult to combine with symmetrical layout.

Sanserif types dispense with the two main distinguishing features of the traditional letterform: the serif and the difference between thick and thin strokes. The result is a loss of interesting detail and that rich texture which makes the roman face so satisfying to design with. This lack of variety within the type mass must be compensated for by a more interesting disposition of these masses on the page. Try substituting a sanserif equivalent for each of the lines in one of your earlier layouts and the monotonous effect will be painfully apparent.

In traditional layout the aim was to create an overall harmony of parts enlivened by contrasting features within. Now the requirement is rather to obtain maximum contrast, preserving some degree of harmony in the interest of unity. The distinction is only one of emphasis, but has far-reaching consequences in practice.

The most essential contrast is of tonal value. Asymmetric design heightens the contrast between white space and print mass in a dramatic way, restoring interest to a sanserif setting. This alone is rarely enough, however, and the contrast between bold and light type is much more vital to sanserif than is the case with roman. In recognition of this, some contemporary grotesques offer more than the customary two weights and the difference between weights is more strongly marked.

As interest has been shifted from within the type mass to the disposition of masses on the page, variety of alphabet loses importance. The Bauhaus typographers, as a natural result of their rationalization plans, tried at one point to dispense with the capital alphabet. The experiment has not met with general approval, but designers ever since have used capitals sparingly—a trend shared by authors and publishers for other reasons and mentioned in section 5. This is particularly so with sanserif, the contemporary typeface, and even lines of capitals are comparatively rare. Compare the two settings here:

76

Publisher's announcement
by Lund Humphries
printed in black

Example of

ROMAN TYPE

Range of sizes and alphabets

example of

sanserif

fewer sizes
one alphabet mainly
more tonal contrast

Sanserifs (with the exception of Monotype Univers) have no small capitals. Letterspacing of sanserif capitals is neither necessary nor desirable, though slight visual letterspacing in large point sizes may be a lesser evil than grossly uneven spacing. Punctuation is more rigorously reduced with sanserif than with roman.

The pioneers of modern design insisted on the recognition of the machine as a factor in production by designing, even when hand setting only was involved, in a mechanical fashion. Sections 31 and 32 explore in detail the influence of typesetting machines on layout, but for the moment it is enough to generalize that in typographic terms, designing in a mechanical way entails keeping to one type family and reducing the number of point sizes used.

Along with the fashion for fewer alphabet changes, these restrictions add to the monotony of a setting. They can be further offset by introducing greater contrast between the fewer sizes of type specified. The subtle gradation of sizes according to the importance of the various parts of the copy, necessary for work in the traditional style, is abandoned and the degree of importance of a line and its logical relationship with other lines is demonstrated rather by its position on the page. Isolation or placing in the main path of the eye emphasizes as effectively as an increase in point size or change of alphabet. Moreover, the far wider choice of position offered by asymmetric design compared to the simple alternative of above or below in symmetry means that relationships between groups can be more subtly suggested. This point will be enlarged upon later.

Practical difficulties arise, of course, when the range of type sizes employed becomes too great, as sizes too large or too small for the estimated reading distance lose legibility. In recent years this fact has sometimes been turned to account by deliberately increasing a main line to an impracticable extent. The reader then becomes aware more of the abstract pattern made by the characters than of the word to be read. This is permissible only when the line does not have to be read quickly and easily, but fulfils primarily a decorative or attention-attracting role. Study the figure below. Deliberate removal of other essentials of legibility, by letter distortion, closing up or even overlapping letters, eliminating interlinear space or other means, most of them made possible by photography in typesetting and printing, will have the same effect and should be confined to similar circumstances.

alpha

large type
as pattern
rather than
readable

very large and
very small types
cannot be read
simultaneously

Prepare a working layout for an invitation card to be printed black on white ivory board, size 90×140mm 3½×5½in). The copy is: 'Group 70 invites you to an exhibition of contemporary sculpture in the Moderna Galleries, Moore Street, from Saturday 20 October to Saturday 3 November, daily 10 am to 8 pm except Sunday/Admission free/ Private view Friday 19 October at pm'. Use one sanserif type family throughout.

On completing this layout, compare with that done after section 18. The difference in typographic treatment is a direct result of the contrast between the contents.

Pages from a booklet
for Stephens Group
printed black and blue

Council of Industrial Design
folder cover
printed black and blue

27 asymmetric rules

Sections 14 and 15 outlined some of the ways in which rules could be used in traditional layout. To learn how rules can be effectively combined with asymmetry, we must examine more closely the nature of straight lines.

The separative effect of a line placed between two elements has already been noted, with the reminder that space often does the job as effectively with less fuss. In addition, it was stated that a straight line is a dominating visual element on the page, taking precedence over the more complex shapes of words, even where the type is heavier.

This has a bearing on the establishment of a horizontal axis in an asymmetric layout. Unless a rule reinforces the type line which forms the axis, it may possibly be seen as a competitor to it, causing ambiguity as to where the main interest is meant to lie. This is the fault in the first figure below. Rules used correctly, as in the other two figures, can support the horizontal axis and lend importance to adjacent type lines, usually for this reason the main line.

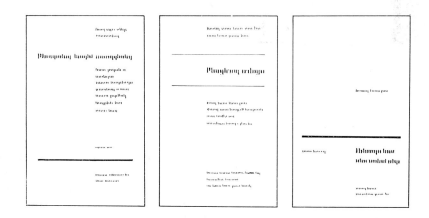

In a few cases rules, though still themselves horizontal, can also reinforce a vertical axis, as in the following figures.

The part played by apparent movement in two-dimensional design ha
already been investigated. Straight lines placed asymmetrically have the sam
property of suggesting movement as do type lines, but to a higher degre
Consider:

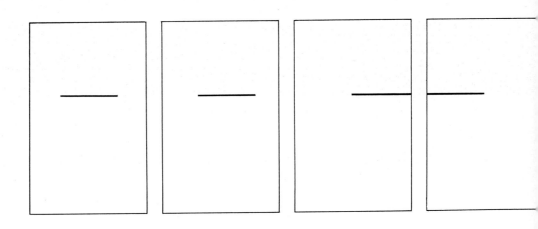

In the first example the line is static. In the next, the eye picks up the line
its left extremity and moves along it to the right. In the third, the moveme
is accelerated by the line actually running off the edge of the paper ('bleeding
Rules bled off one edge are usually best kept to right-hand positions; othe
wise, as in the final diagram shown, the eye is left in mid-air. Right-to-le
movement, as was discovered in section 23, is unlikely to be induced, as it
contrary to our reading habits. One of the figures above does in fact sho
a successful layout involving rules placed to the left.

As a right-hand bleed inevitably takes the eye right off the edge of the page, the device can only be employed when this is intended, as in booklet covers, where the aim is to make the reader turn over the page. It makes no sense in letterheadings, cards and such one-sided, self-contained work.

Council of Industrial Design

**Services
for the
Engineering
Industries**

Council of Industrial Design
folder printed black and blue
on cover and page 3
black and brown on page 2

Council of Industrial Design

CHAIRMAN SIR DUNCAN OPPENHEIM
DIRECTOR MR PAUL REILLY

The CoID with its Scottish Committee was established in 1944 by the Coalition Government, 'to promote by all practicable means the improvement of design in the products of British industry'.
It receives an annual grant from Government funds and currently earns an income amounting to eighty per cent of that grant.
The CoID's policy is directed by twenty-six Council Members representing industry, commerce, industrial design and education, and its activities include:

assistance to manufacturers on problems of industrial design

discussion of these problems by means of conferences, courses and lectures

recommendation of qualified industrial designers to industry

display of well designed consumer products in the permanent but constantly changing exhibition at THE DESIGN CENTRE

other displays, both at home and abroad, to promote well designed British goods

publication of DESIGN magazine which provides information on all aspects of design in industry

The CoID's services for the engineering industries have one basic purpose: to help improve design in engineering as it affects the user.
This purpose lies within the aims of industrial design. Form, texture and colour, the industrial designer's media, can be manipulated to ease operation, to simplify complexity, to demonstrate such qualities as efficiency and precision, and to make machines and equipment appropriate to modern surroundings. Design in this context is an essential counterpart to technical development—a developing sales factor especially in overseas markets. For the buyer it may be a deciding factor.

In traditional work the overriding principle was one of harmony, and this was reflected in our insistence on a close correlation between weight of rules and type in such layouts. Now, on the contrary, the principle is one of contrast and this must extend to the specification of rules, which should be markedly lighter or bolder than the accompanying type.

In contemporary industrial design, decoration is entirely lacking. It is excluded by a doctrine typical of our time which says that form should be determined by the way the object is going to be used, secondarily by the nature of the materials it is made of and the economic methods of manufacture. In terms of typography, this means that the straight line is to be used not for its decorative properties, but for its ability to separate, emphasize and indicate direction, as an aid to understanding the copy. The composite rule is decorative and is not favoured in modern design, being replaced by the single functional rule. Stylistically, the single rule matches the monotone nature of sanserif, as can be appreciated here:

sans

contrasting
rule
directs
attention
to type

sanserif

**sans
serif**

Prepare a working layout for a booklet cover, size 200×125mm (8×5in), the copy being: 'The automation of power stations/English Electronic'. Use a sanserif type and incorporate one or more rules.

In the illustration under, rules have been introduced in logical places to divide the page area horizontally in an interesting way, as discussed on page 73.

Title page
of exhibition catalogue
for Arts Council
of Great Britain

Eardley

The Scottish Committee
of the Arts Council of Great Britain

Joan Eardley R.S.A. (1921-1963)

A memorial exhibition

25 January - 22 February 1964
The Art Gallery and Museum
Kelvingrove Glasgow

29 February - 14 March 1964
The Diploma Galleries of the Royal Scottish Academy
The Mound Edinburgh

A shortened version of this exhibition
will subsequently be on tour

28 choosing the paper

The varieties of papers and boards discussed in this section, together with details of their manufacture and the terms in use to describe them are set out in Clowes: *A guide to printing*. British Standard 3203:1964 also contains useful information, being a glossary of paper, stationery and allied terms. Paper manufacturers provide information on their products which can be procured without difficulty.

The most important factor influencing the designer in his choice of stock is price. A current copy of the Lund Humphries periodical *Paper facts and figures* is indispensable.

Apart from cost, the vital consideration in choosing paper for a job is purpose. How is the job to be handled, used and read? For example, a poster which is to be pasted up must be machine glazed on one side only, the other being rough for better adhesion. Paper which is to be written on with an ordinary pen should be fairly smooth and heavily sized in comparison with printing papers. For easy readability of extensive text matter a glossy paper should be avoided, as should too brilliant a white. There are many more obvious instances of the influence of purpose on paper choice.

Durability must be considered, too. Generally speaking, the more resistant a paper is to chemical deterioration and tearing, the more it costs. The paper selected should have only the strength and likely length of life appropriate to the particular work. There is no point in specifying a relatively expensive woodfree for a handbill which is thrown away immediately after being read. An account, however, which may be expected to be filed away for some time and which may have to withstand repeated handling, needs more lasting qualities.

The weight, bulk and opacity of paper are qualities worthy of attention. They are related but not necessarily directly proportional. A bulky paper is not always heavier than a thin paper and, although bulkiness and heaviness increase opacity, they are by no means the only factors operative. A heavy paper normally costs more than one similar but lighter, yet will be preferred when strength and a substantial appearance are wanted, the general public tending to equate quality with thickness of sheet. Bulky papers are often selected for that reason and also to make a job of few pages seem more, but this cannot be reckoned as good design. More often, reduction in bulk is desired, perhaps to make the job fit more easily into an envelope. Reduction in weight is always wanted when postage rates are a consideration. Opacity is important whenever the sheet is to be printed both sides, or is followed by another printed page. Too translucent a sheet allows the print on the back or on the page beneath to show through, with detriment both to legibility and appearance.

The suitability of the stock for printing and allied processes can be competently judged only by the printer. Selections of paper and board should be confirmed by him before committing the client to expense. With growing experience, however, the designer will begin to know what can safely be specified, the snags likely to occur and when it is better to consult the printer.

The main considerations are these. To begin with, paper surface must suit the production processes. Though today there are few limitations imposed by any method of printing, additional work such as embossing, creasing, folding stapling and perforating achieve varying degrees of success with different stock. Choice of paper surface is also conditioned by demands made by colour printing (see section 21), and illustration by line and tone (see sections 46 and 48).

The effect of paper surface on the printed appearance of type is most important in the case of letterpress, where the pressing of the inked character into the paper results in a thickening and blunting of the printed image. The rougher and softer the stock, the more obvious the distortion. With coated papers, on the other hand, where ideally no indentation of the surface is made hardly any thickening of the original image takes place.

Most book faces were designed to allow for this thickening and consequently look weak, oversharp and meagre when printed on coateds. Plantin is an example of a text face specifically designed for coated papers, having the thickening effect already incorporated into it. As a guide, it is approximately true to say that old face types look their best on papers which have been only lightly calendered. Transitionals and moderns retain their characteristic sharpness of cut, without undue loss of legibility due to dazzle, on more heavily calendered uncoated surfaces. Only a few traditional types have been recut for use on coated stock, although slabserif and sanserif are eminently suitable. In the larger sizes of type the effects of paper surface are negligible and can be ignored except in extreme cases, such as fat face on art paper. Consult Dowding: *Factors in the choice of type faces* for a thorough analysis of this problem.

Finally, choice of stock is, after all other factors have been taken into account, a matter of aesthetic preference. Quality of paper adds to or detracts from the status of the printed word. Evenness of surface texture and colour and even disposition of fibre, without undue specks or blotches when looked through against the light, together with pleasant handling properties, are the marks of a good quality paper, from a purely aesthetic viewpoint. Comparative whiteness, where a good white is wanted, is also worth checking.

The feel and appearance of a sheet can occasionally be employed as qualities in themselves to supplement copy and layout in communicating the message to the reader. A hard, glossy, brilliant coated gives a different impression from a warm, pleasant and comfortable antique laid. Each can be used profitably in its correct context, though it must be said that cost, printability and the other considerations touched on above often decide for the designer. For example, a suitable choice of stock for the exercise in section 5 might be Grosvenor, Chater & Co Ltd's 'Curzon' cover, white, 150 gsm.

In *Paper facts and figures* this cover paper is listed as being available in several alternative full sheet sizes, which is the case with most papers. The dimensions quoted are British Standard and the complete list of names with their metric and inch equivalents is easily obtainable. Choice among them is determined by the need to cut the full sheet to the finished size of the job with the least possible waste offcut.

It is therefore common to use actual sub-divisions of the standard sizes when settling the finished dimensions of the page. The diagram shows that sub-divisions such as folio and quarto have no equivalent in inches until the standard sheet (broadside) is identified. Thus Crown (381×508mm or 15×20in) octavo is 191×127mm or 7½×5in, but Royal (508×635mm or 20×25in) octavo is 254×158mm or 10×6¼in.

In practice it is inadvisable to specify the exact sub-division of the parent sheet as the final size of the job. Even with work comprising only a single leaf, it is better to trim the edges before or after printing. The typographer must therefore work to a finished size at least 3mm (⅛in) less on each of the four sides. When bleed is asked for anywhere in the layout, 6mm (¼in) trim all round is the practice.

Machine grip must also be considered. Small jobbing such as we have dealt with exclusively in exercises to date is habitually gripped at the shorter side, in upright work always at the head rather than the tail. At this edge there must be a minimum of 12mm (½in) unprinted paper for the grippers on the machine to hold during printing. If, owing to the design, this space is not available, the paper has to be cut larger and the unwanted part trimmed off afterwards. This means that the maximum final size of the job is further reduced.

Normal trim, bleed and machine grip all affect the largest size of sheet which can be economically obtained from standard ream sizes. When, as often, it is left to the designer to decide the dimensions of the job, it cannot be too strongly urged that this should be worked out from available standard ream sizes of the chosen paper, taking into account all of these contributory factors.

To return to the exercise from section 5, we find that white Curzon cover is procurable in cover Royal (520×647mm or 20½×25½in) which offers six 200×250mm (8×10in) 4pp covers out of each sheet with minimal waste and allowing for trim. No problem of grip arises.

Two further points deserve attention. Watermarked papers should be cut out of the sheet so that the watermark is right way up with the print. This is a possible limitation, as is the printer's requirement that the grain of the paper in large sheets, especially where register work is involved, should run in the same direction as the feed.

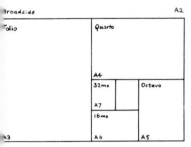

Broadside
Folio
Quarto
A2
A4
32mo
Octavo
A7
16mo
A3
A6
A5

Trim on single sheet:

3mm approximately
6mm approximately on bled work

Go back over all the exercises which you have done and write down details of the paper or board most suitable in each instance. One or more comprehensive paper specimen books such as are issued by the larger papermakers or merchants are essential help in finding the correct stock for the work. Make a note of the maker's name and write a full description, including ream size and weight in lb, substance in gsm and colour, on each layout. Comparative prices may be checked in *Paper facts and figures*.

86

If facilities are available, proof a paragraph set in various text types on newsprint, book paper, calendered printing, supercalendered and coated papers. Compare the results. Failing this, begin a collection of printed samples of the same and different typefaces printed on these papers.

International standard sizes are sometimes used in preference to British Standard. It must be clearly understood that the international A sizes refer to the trimmed, finished job and not to the paper as supplied originally to the printer. As it is the end product which is standard, an appropriate size of full sheet must be ordered to allow for the necessary trim and perhaps machine grip. Either a suitable British Standard ream or one of the A-based sizes (RA or SRA) stocked in certain papers can be used for this. At present the main employment of international sizes is in the fields of stationery and all envelope inserts, magazines and catalogues, particularly loose-leaf.

While continuing to work through this book, find out as much as you can about paper, its manufacture, varieties and uses. Gain as much experience of handling paper as possible, identifying it, estimating its weight and testing if possible its influence on type and colour.

29 stationery

The design of stationery poses a fresh problem for the typographer. Until now he could be sure that he was in complete control of the appearance of the finished job, but with stationery the job is in most cases not complete until either typing or writing has been added to it. The way to tackle such a problem is to decide first of all what areas of space are to be allocated to subsequent typing or writing, then to lay out the print in the remaining space in such a way that the position of such additions is determined as far as possible.

Little commercial stationery today is handwritten, so this contingency can be disposed of with the observation that in such an event dotted lines (leaders) or fine rules are necessary as guide lines, unless the paper is already feint ruled. No such lines should ever be specified for the typewriter.

The main aesthetic problem faced by the designer of stationery is how to reconcile printed and typewritten letters. Since it is clearly impossible to conceal the difference, it is better to accept it and honestly contrast the two. Types reminiscent of typewriter, and in the same size, should be avoided.

On the other hand, total incompatibility between print and typing is un-desirable, and it is worth recalling the facts that the typewriter ranges its lines at the beginning but not at the end and that it is tedious, though not impossible, to centre lines on each other. It follows that asymmetrically designed print accompanies typing more naturally than centred layouts. This is not to claim that symmetrical design is entirely out of place in stationery, for many splendid examples exist, but they are exceptions where the nature of the copy has demanded traditional treatment for expressive purposes.

The most common and important item of stationery is the letterheading. Other items are dealt with later in the book. In accordance with the above principles let us first of all take a sheet of trimmed Large Post quarto (250 × 200mm or 10 × 8in) and indicate on it where the principal typewritten matter will lie.

The first thing which a typist will do is set the left-hand margin on the machine, about 25mm or 1in from the edge of the paper. Draw here a vertical line the full length of the sheet. In commercial correspondence the addressee's name and address have to appear, more often before the letter than after, though figs. 3 and 4 demonstrate this other possibility. Allow space for four or five lines (ems) beginning at most 70mm or 2½in from the top of the sheet.

The date is commonly placed at the right, about 70mm or 2½in from the right-hand edge to leave room for the longest date, and space is saved if it is made to share a line with the recipient's name, as in the first two of the following figures. At least one reference number has to be allowed for, either customarily preceding the rest of the typing, as in three of these figures, or sharing a line with the recipient's address as in the first, again to save space.

88

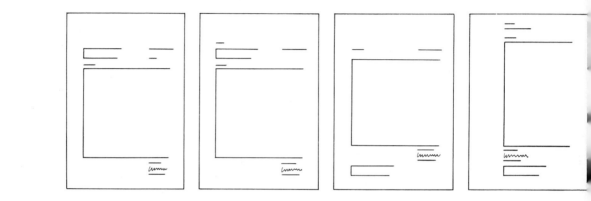

Below the letter itself, 'yours faithfully', signature and designation can be lined up with the date at a satisfactory minimum distance from the foot, taking into account the typewriter's inability to type on the last 20mm. The maximum length of the actual letter can then be gauged. The first three figures show conventional typing layouts modified to bring them in line with contemporary trends in typography, while the last represents an unusual but feasible alternative.

Archaic practices such as progressively increasing indentions in addresses and excessive, pedantic punctuation are still unfortunately taught in typing schools. Where opportunity arises, typists should be instructed to conform to a reasonable style. Layouts for customer submission must always be typed in a correct style to show the total effect of the letterheading in action. This acts as a guide to typists, too. Revise the advice offered at the end of section 10 regarding correct punctuation.

It is clear from the full-scale drawing you have made that the space reserved for the printed heading is very shallow. The commonest error in the design of letterheadings is failure to appreciate this, resulting in insufficient space being left for even an average length letter. Observe too that this space is much longer than it is deep, so as well as the need to economise in depth, it is most desirable to have the layout fill the whole width comfortably. This is done by strengthening the horizontal axis, but revise section 6 on the relation between alphabet choice and available space, section 11 on choice of typeface for a given area, and look at the examples in section 24, showing alternative ways of creating a vertical axis, noting which suits best a wide format.

The average printed letterheading contains the firm's name, possibly a description of the kind of business carried on, the address, telephone number and telegraphic address. Other information may be added: directors' names, for instance. Type sizes are always dictated by reading distance and modified by the relative importance of parts of the copy to the reader. Since letters are held at normal reading distance of 18 inches or so, the basic sizes are those proper to books: 9pt to 12pt. Two groups are excepted. The firm's name is the main line and may have to be identified in a file at arm's length, so it goes in a larger size. It must remain readable at closer range, however, which severely restricts the increase. Any subsidiary information such as names of directors or date of establishment is not meant to be read except by those specifically searching for it, so can be relegated to the smallest practicable point size.

As regards print layout, a look back at your sketch of the typescript will reveal that a vertical axis already exists at a satisfactory point, determined by the date line. If this is extended upwards, it can be utilized as the vertical axis for the printed heading, integrating print and typing. The main line receives due prominence if it is isolated on the left of this axis, itself forming the horizontal axis. Address, telephone and telegram are expected on the right, together and probably in the same type size, since today they are of equal importance. Miscellaneous information conforms to the axes, taking into account the logical order of reading. Copy placed in the space to the left gains importance, while copy appearing above the main line and to the right is out of the reading-line.

In a specific project, the amount and nature of the wording to a large extent dictates the final layout and the above analysis is not meant as more than a guide to the kind of thinking required. Radically different designs can evolve as naturally from the same typewritten style and from as logical an appraisal of the copy supplied. Study the following examples, each a solution to a specific problem:

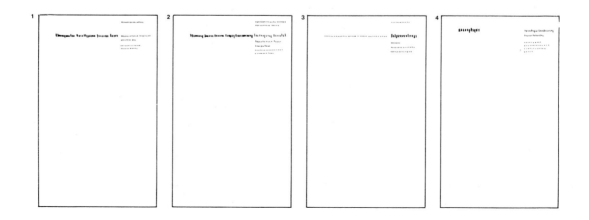

90

In every case a 'setting-line' has been provided for the left-hand edge of the typescript, lining up with the extreme left of the printed heading and leaving an adequate margin. Now attempt these exercises, completing each layout by typing a specimen letter on it. Specify papers, envelopes and inks. A list of

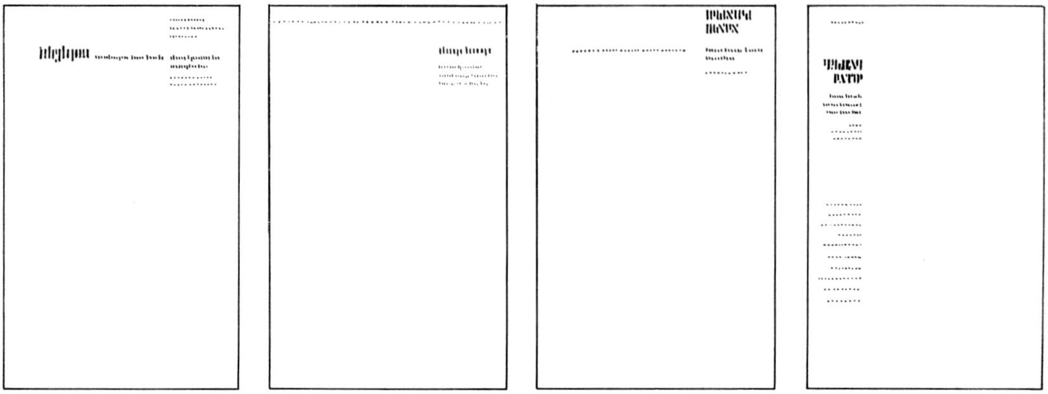

Letterheadings
for Kodak
die-stamped in red and black
and for Balding & Mansell
printed grey, orange and black

Prepare a working layout, after doing a number of sketches to a reduced scale, for a British Standard quarto letterheading, printed in one working. The copy is: 'Confederated Ironfounders Limited, Domestic Appliance Division, Bournville Road, Sudbury, Middlesex/Telephone 0932–76543/London showrooms: 82 Brown Street, W1Q 7CH'.

Design a letterheading to be printed in two workings, size A4, for 'International Festival of the Arts/ Festival office: 11 Oxbridge Road, London W1A 3PQ/Telephone 01–387 2456/Chairman: The Right Honourable Sir James Duncan, M.C, T.D./Festival director: Peter Weiss/Secretary: Graham Williams'.

international standard envelopes appears in Biggs: *Basic typography*. The C6 and C5/6 (DL) sizes come within the Post Office Preferred limits.

Window envelopes, with a transparent panel or an aperture, avoid the necessity of typing the address on the envelope, but it is essential that the precise limits within which the address must be typed are indicated on the letterheading. The conventional method is by four L-shaped pieces of type, each on an em body, but a rectangle of fine rule, perhaps in colour, or some other equally effective means can be devised. For the purpose of the last exercise assume that this area is 95mm ($3\frac{3}{4}$in) long by 30mm ($1\frac{1}{4}$in) deep and is situated 20mm ($\frac{3}{4}$in) from the left-hand edge of the sheet and 40mm ($1\frac{1}{2}$in) from the top.

91

The precise indication of where reference numbers and date are to be typed to conform to the print can be achieved by including the words 'Our ref, your ref, date'. When window envelopes are used this is most desirable. Consult British Standards 1808 Part 1:1963 and study these examples before commencing the final exercise:

Window envelope for Balding & Mansell printed orange and grey to match the letterheading illustrated on page 90

Prepare a caseroom layout for a letterheading to suit a C5/6 window envelope, 110×220mm ($4\frac{1}{4}×8\frac{5}{8}$in), printed in black and one other colour, for 'Carchester College of Art/ Principal: A. M. Hurst/George Fourth Street, Carchester 8/Telephone 012–33456/Our ref: /Your ref: /Date:'.

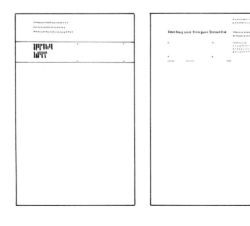

92

5 Hanway Place London W1P 9DF 01-636 2596

habitat

Habitat Designs Limited Directors: Terence Conran Caroline Conran John Mawer JR Beevor FCA MA DB Phillips Secretary: A Mitra

Habitat Designs Limited
5 Hanway Place London W1P 9DF 01 636 2596

habitat

Habitat Designs Limited
5 Hanway Place London W1 MUSeum 2596

habitat

with compliments

Letterheading, envelope,
label and compliments slip
printed orange and black
for Habitat

habitat

30 house style

A firm's stationery can be a useful instrument in its public relations. A good   93
typographer must be able to present the 'image' or personality which a firm
wishes to project by intelligent design of its stationery. This image is most
effective and memorable when the same basic design idea is adapted to meet
the particular functional requirements of each item. This is known as creating
a 'house style'.

To begin with, the designer must find out what kind of image the firm
would like to present to the recipients of its communications. This may be
partly discoverable from the copy itself: nature of product or service in
particular. But it is always advisable to talk with the client, and if possible
with key staff members, to elicit from them just what qualities should be
emphasized: modernity, efficiency, long establishment, exclusiveness or
whatever. The sketches for a range of stationery in house style below are for
an imaginary graphic design group, therefore a sophisticated, fashionable style
is obligatory. Observe the strong family resemblance between items and how
the same idea has been adapted to suit each. If a colour is introduced it will
be the same, or related, in all:

British Standard 1808, part 1:1963 and Henrion and Parkins: *Design co-
ordination and corporate image* should be consulted before proceeding with the
exercise.

94

Formulate a house style comprising letterheading, envelope, invoice, statement, compliments slip, business card and label for a printer who wishes to establish a reputation for good quality work and who offers a design consultant service. The basic copy is: 'Stylprint Limited/designers and printers/Head office: 28 Albemarle Street, London E1C 5AR/Telephone 01–387 1234/Telex 56789/Works: Caxton Works, 150 Mary Street, High Wycombe, Buckinghamshire/ Telephone 0494–1234'.

Prepare working layouts for each of the items of stationery, using appropriate A sizes and not more than two workings in any one item. On the layouts or on proofs or photostats of them, type specimen wording in appropriate places. Before producing any working layouts, make thumbnail sketches of all to check that the basic house style idea is fully capable of development. All forms should have, like the letterheading, a left-hand filing margin of about 25mm or 1in.

Letterheading: As this is the most important visually, begin with roughs of letterheadings in both A4 and A5 sizes. Note that although international A sizes should always be preferred for stationery, their adoption depends on the sizes of existing filing cabinets and office equipment in the firm.

Envelope: A printed matching envelope of suitable size to accommodate the letterheading with convenient folding, chosen from the international C range is required. Compare the whiteness of paper and envelope. Post Office regulations forbid printing on the right-hand half of the envelope face. Copy is limited to the firm's name, business and head office address, without telephone or telex.

Invoice: This is sent to a purchaser about the same time as the order is delivered, giving details of the order and listing the price. The invoice reproduces the letterheading with the addition of something like the following wording: 'Invoice' prominently displayed but still secondary to the firm's name; 'Order no.' placed as early as possible; 'Delivery address' heading the space allotted to the addressee in the letterheading; 'Your order   date   ' and 'Carriage   , deliver by   ' preceding the main body of the

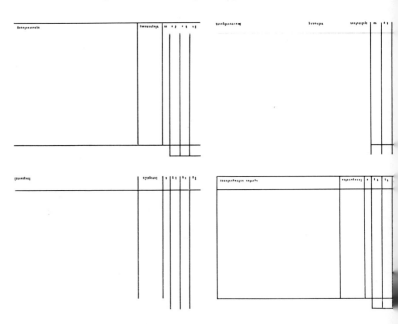

invoice. This main part consists of columns defined by vertical rules at appropriate widths to accommodate typing which is to appear under these headings: 'Item/Quantity/Code/Debit/Credit/Total'. A horizontal rule cuts off this area from the heading proper and another may possibly be put across the foot of the area, where a grand total has to be provided for in each of the three money columns. In the present instance this rule is desirable, since the words 'Special instructions' are to be printed under the ruled-off area, with sufficient space for a few lines of typing. But an absolute minimum of rules should be indicated, in accordance with modern usage and to avoid confusion. Sections 33 and 34 enlarge on this point. Consider the treatments of the main typing area shown opposite and study fig. 3 in British Standard 1808:1963.

Statement: The statement of account is dispatched to the customer monthly and though again based on the letterheading, may be A5 size, in which case type sizes may have to be slightly reduced and the layout adapted. Note that with international paper sizes, subdivisions retain the same proportions. Here the word 'Statement' receives similar treatment to 'Invoice' in the previous job. The space for the addressee is restored precisely as in the letterheading, followed by the line: 'in account with Stylprint Limited'. The new headings for the body are: 'Order no./Date/Quantity/Ref' and a repeat of the three money columns with totals. Along the foot of the sheet incorporate 'Terms: $2\frac{1}{2}\%$ discount for settlement within 28 days of invoice'. See fig. 7 in British Standard 1808:1963.

Compliments slip: This is formal and unemphatic, of a size suitable for placing inside an envelope without more than one fold, yet large enough to be noticed when included in a parcel—A6 is suggested. The discreet line 'With compliments' precedes the rest of the copy, which is an abbreviated version of the letterheading—say, without the works address.

Business card: Even more formal and restrained, and of a size which fits the pocket book but will not be lost in a file, the business card is the personal card of an executive or representative of the firm. The same copy is used as for the compliments slip, save that 'With compliments' is replaced by the name and position of the card's owner: for example 'J. G. Smith/Managing director'.

Label: This is printed on gummed paper with a view to sticking on parcels and large envelopes. Because such a label must deliver its message over a greater distance than the other stationery, larger type sizes combined with a much bolder treatment are demanded. Space for typing the addressee's particulars should be indicated first and the print in house style disposed in the remaining space. Select A5 or A6 size. Copy is identical to the letterheading. *The Post Office Guide* recommends that printed wording other than the address of the recipient should be confined to the left-hand half of the label, but many designers appear not to accept this limitation.

Specify all papers, boards, envelopes and inks.

Richard Hamilton

11 Photograph of a working drawing for **Pin-up**
1960–61 (**D**)
(Robert Fraser Gallery, London)

A working drawing made while the painting
was well under way to solve the problem of
the blank right hand side of the composition.

12 Sketch for **Hugh Gaitskell as a Famous
Monster of Filmland** relief 1963 (**E**) and
painting 1964 (**F**)

The drawing from a coarse half-tone press
cutting was made originally for the relief (in
its first state an oil study with a copper under-
painting, but the oil paint became affected by
the priming and was later removed leaving the
study in its present condition). It was only at a
later stage that Hamilton decided to use the
photograph itself blown up to form a photographic base for the painting. This was the
first painting he made with a total use of
photography; previously he had only amal-
gamated photographs into paintings in the
form of collage.

13 Study for **Interior** 1964 (**G**) and **Interior II**
1964–65 (**H**)
(Lent by Sir Roland Penrose, London)

The composition was originally based on a still
from a film called *Shockproof* taken with a
wide angle lens which seemed to distort the
perspective. This is one of three collage
studies experimenting with various elements
common to the composition — a figure,
pictures, curtains, interior furnishings in
general — and in particular exploring further
the mood ('ominous, provocative, ambigu-
ous') and the perspective effects suggested by
the original photograph. Other studies for the
pictures include a working drawing for the
desk in **Interior** (private collection, Ulm)
which was made on a printed perspective
grid and blown up photographically to the size
of the painting.

E **Study for Portrait of Hugh Gaitskell
as a Famous Monster of Filmland**
1963
Metallic paint on relief panel
46 × 46 cm / 18 × 18 in
Robert Fraser Gallery, London

F **Portrait of Hugh Gaitskell as a
Famous Monster of Filmland** 1964
Oil and collage on photograph on panel
61 × 61 cm / 24 × 24 in
Arts Council of Great Britain

G **Interior** 1964
Oil, collage, cellulose, fablon, mirror,
pencil, silkscreen
122 × 163 cm / 48 × 64 in
Robert Fraser Gallery, London

H **Interior II** 1964–65
Oil, collage, cellulose, metal relief on panel
122 × 163 cm / 48 × 64 in
Tate Gallery, London

David Hockney

1937 Born Bradford
1953–57 Studied at Bradford School of Art
1959–62 Studied at Royal College of Art
1961–63 In New York, Berlin, Italy and Egypt
1963 Taught at University of Iowa
1965 At University of Colorado, USA
At present lives in Los Angeles

Although David Hockney sometimes paints a
picture from memory without reference to
drawings, generally he does a good deal of
drawing. When he feels like drawing he tends
to do so for a few days, and from the results
will pick out some drawings to develop into
paintings.

He may draw out of his head, from nature or
from photographs of all kinds, but he does not
pay much attention to the drawings themselves while painting. However, sometimes
when a painting is already in progress he will
make more drawings for it. And generally if he
is using photographs makes a drawing first to
simplify the image so that he can remember it.
He sometimes paints from nature, but only
details of a composition; he never paints a
whole picture in this way.

He now finds that he is painting without
making drawings more frequently. Cases in
point have been his **Still-life** series, 1965, and
**Picture of the Rocky Mountains with
Tired Indians**, 1965 (Peter Stuyvesant
Foundation) a painting done in Colorado, in
the middle of the Rockies, though the
mountains in the picture were made up.

1 Study for **The First Marriage** 1962 (**A**)
(Lent by Mrs Dorothy Morland, London)

The painting was inspired by the sight of a
friend standing beside an Egyptian sculpture
in a museum in East Berlin; from a distance
the two figures looked like a couple posing for
a wedding photograph — a marriage of styles,
the stylized Egyptian figure with the real
human one. Hockney made two or three
drawings in Berlin but the picture was painted
on his return to London.

A **The First Marriage** 1962
Oil on canvas
183 × 213 cm / 72 × 84 in
Tate Gallery, London

Pages from exhibition catalogue
for Arts Council of Great Britain

Mechanical methods of typesetting can save time and money and are employed whenever technically and economically feasible. Such systems, however, impose certain limitations on the designer which must be known if he is to take account of them. This section examines the implications of the Monotype single-type mechanical composing system; line composition is dealt with in the next section. Technical descriptions of composing machines can be obtained from the companies and are briefly given in Clowes: *A guide to printing*. Here we are concerned only with their influence on the design of print. 97

The Monotype system produces lines of composed type matter up to a maximum 60 em measure, normally in body sizes from 5 to 14pt. The greatest limitation of the system is its inability to change the body size or face of the type without expensive delay. Thus its economic use is confined to quantities of lines of the same point size and face. Where a design consists, as has been the case in our examples so far, of lines of type varying in point size and sometimes face, setting by Monotype machine is impractical.

Lines of varying measure present no special difficulties, because all can be set to the longest measure and the excess blanks thrown away at the make-up stage.

There is a limit to the number of characters of the chosen type face and size which are available for composition at any one time. The lay of the diecase is to a certain extent flexible, but with a normal text type only seven alphabets are accommodated, together with one or two sets of figures. Should special sorts be wanted, it may be impossible to maintain this maximum. Characters occurring infrequently can of course be added afterwards by hand, and quantities of lines in other alphabets, typefaces or sizes may be set separately and inserted later in the proper places. If this additional matter is to share a line with the original setting, expensive rejustification by hand cannot be avoided.

The reason for the provision of bold type in small sizes can now be appreciated. They lend emphasis and distinctiveness to a heading either on its own or within a text line, without the uneconomic change to a larger type. When designing for Monotype, careful and extensive use of the available alphabets in the diecase, in order of relative emphasis, is obligatory. The order of decreasing emphasis is given opposite for reference, though the use of all seven in headings in one job is certainly not recommended.

BOLD CAPITALS

Bold lowercase

ROMAN CAPITALS

ITALIC CAPITALS

SMALL CAPITALS

Italic lowercase

Roman lowercase

Letterspacing of capitals and small capitals is accomplished on Monotype by increasing the width of the body of characters by one, two or three units, two being the most commonly used:

ONE UNIT LETTERSPACED   ONE UNIT LETTERSPACED

TWO UNIT LETTERSPACED   TWO UNIT LETTERSPACED

THREE UNIT LETTERSPACED   THREE UNIT LETTERSPACED

Some knowledge of the Monotype set-width system is desirable at this stage, though its full implications for the typographer do not become apparent until section 33, which deals with tabular setting. Set-width is explained in Monotype publications; it should be understood that the alphabet length of a typeface with a set-width of $9\frac{1}{2}$ will be less than that of one having a set-width of 10, and that set-width changes with typeface and body size. The point to grasp is that the em-quad of a fount of $9\frac{1}{2}$ set is $9\frac{1}{2}$pts wide, irrespective of the point size of the type.

The typographer may in some cases have to allow for this, for example: 'indent 6 ems o/b' (own body) means six em-quads of the set of the fount in use. In the case of a fount of 10pt, $9\frac{1}{2}$ set, the indention would measure six times $9\frac{1}{2}$pts, *not* six times 10pts. In general, measurements of this nature within the type line are given in ems o/b, while overall measures continue of course to be in 12pt ems.

Leading between lines of text composition, provided it is the same throughout, can be added on the machine. Usually it is found simpler to cast the type on a body of increased point size. The appearance when printed is identical, for example: 10pt, 2pt leaded, is the same as 10pt cast on a 12pt body (10/12pt).

When designing for mechanical composition it becomes necessary to calculate the number of lines which the copy will make when set in the chosen type size, face and alphabet, to a given measure. First count the number of characters (spaces and punctuation are counted as characters) in the copy. Then check how many characters of the chosen fount will be contained on average in the measure, either by reference to Monotype copyfitting tables or by counting against a typical line in a specimen setting. The total characters in the copy, divided by the estimated characters in one type line, gives the number of lines when set.

The short lines at ends of paragraphs introduce a complication. In calculations which have to be very accurate, do a separate sum for every paragraph. When the copy is too extensive for this, count short lines in the copy as if they were full lines.

Lines ranged to the left, like centred lines, offer no problems in the setting. The less conventional ranging to the right has to be done by the operator and takes more time. Unjustified lines, that is, flush left, ragged right, are often to be preferred in asymmetric layout when the text is short.

The unevenness of the right-hand margin relieves the rigidity of straight line forms and word spacing is naturally even. Shorter measures and increased leading may be needed to restore full legibility.

When marking up copy for such fixed-space setting it is advisable to stipulate whether word-breaks are to be avoided or not. In the former case, recommended when copy is short and the resulting unevenness of line ends not unsightly, the average number of characters contained in a line will be slightly less than the figure given in copyfitting tables. Hyphenation minimises the raggedness of the right-hand edge and is particularly necessary in short measures. There is then little or no effect on copyfitting.

Paragraphs are marked by a one-em indent, save at the opening paragraph which is always full out, or alternatively by additional space between them. So a typical mark-up instruction for Monotype text might be: '10/12pt Times rom, ranged left, unjustified right with normal word-breaks, set to 18 ems. Indent 1 em o/b at paras, first para full out'.

It is also essential to mark up the copy itself. This should be typewritten double-spaced on one side only of quarto sheets for the operator's convenience. Copy which is difficult to read for any reason should be retyped in this manner. The operator consults the layout before beginning to set, to familiarize himself with the general instructions, but details of style must be indicated on the copy. Punctuation, spelling and capitalization must be standardized and alphabet changes marked in the recognized code:

italic   small capitals   roman capitals   bold   bold capitals

British Standard proof-readers' marks should be used for further indications of style. British Standard 1219:1958 contains the list of these.

Prepare a working layout for an advertisement, area 36 ems deep by 24 ems, to be inserted in a weekly newspaper set in Monotype Times series. The copy is: 'Oxbridge University Press/Sales representative /620 characters of text/Apply to: the Office Manager, Oxbridge University Press/Barclay House, 20 Euston Road, London W1R 8AQ'. A composite rule border around the full area is asked for. Economic reasons dictate the minimum use of hand setting.

Design an octavo pamphlet, precise size to be decided, printed one side only in black and a colour, copy being: 'A career in the bank/Never before have opportunities for young people been as promising as they are today in Bartons Bank. Here is a brief outline of the career that awaits you there/For ambitious young men (710 characters text follow)/And there's scope for girls as well (280 characters text follow)/Write for further particulars to the Staff Managers, 45 Lombard Street, Manchester M6 2RR/ Bartons Bank'. Make a working layout and specify paper and inks.

LEICESTER COLLEGE OF ART

22 The Private Press at Gregynog
By J. Michael Davies. Leicester, 1959.
Designed by the author. Lithographed illustrations by
Rigby Graham.

J. H. MASON

23 Cupid and Psyche
Translated by J. H. Mason. London, 1935.
Woodcuts by Vivien Gribble. No. 76 of 'about 130 copies'.
(Mason was formerly compositor at the Doves Press.
See No. 11).

MERIDIAN PRESS   *Alvin Badenhop*

24 Ouarzazate: the Kasbah in the Desert
By Alvin Badenhop. Hauula, Hawaii, 1959.
Designed and illustrated with linocuts by the author.
No. 113 of 240 copies.

MERRION PRESS   *Susan Mahon*

25 Wolperiana, an illustrated guide to Berthold L. Wolpe
With various observations by Charles Mozley;
introduced by E. M. Hatt. London, 1960.
Designed by Susan Mahon.

MINIATURE PRESS   *John Ryder*

26 Miniature Folio of Private Presses
Organised by John Ryder. London, 1960.
A co-operative effort containing 28 sections, each of
which consists of 4 pages (some French-folded)
printed at the presses concerned, and gathered loosely in
a case. One of 100 copies.

MELCHIOR W. MITTL

27 Orpheus and Eurydice
By Publius Ovidius Naso. Mindelheim, Bayern, 1961.
Illustrated with five wood engravings by
Hans Orlowski. No. 114 of 133 copies.

NONESUCH PRESS   *Francis Meynell*

28 Nonesuch Dickensiana
Prospectus for the famous 'Nonesuch Dickens', published
in 23 volumes in 1938. London, 1937.
Designed by Francis Meynell; printed commercially.

29 Poems and Pieces 1911 to 1961
By Francis Meynell. London, 1961.
Designed by Francis Meynell; printed at the Stellar Press.
Out of series copy: edition limited to 750 copies.

ORIOLE PRESS   *Joseph Ishill*

30 William Caxton
By Holbrook Jackson. Berkeley Heights, New Jersey,
1959.
Designed by Joseph Ishill. No. 83 of 220 copies.

PANDORA PRESS   *Toni Savage*

31 Lines Written among the Euganean Hills
By Percy Bysshe Shelley. Leicester, 1961.
Designed by Toni Savage; drawings by Rigby Graham.
Out of series copy: edition limited to 60 copies.

PERCIVAL & GRAHAM
                George Percival and Rigby Graham

32 The Nightingale and The Rose
A fairy tale by Oscar Wilde. Leicester, 1961.
Designed by Percival and Graham;
privately printed by the Cistercian Monks of
Mount Saint Bernard Abbey. One of 'a few copies only'.

PIGEONHOLE PRESS   *Ray Dilley*

33 James Johnston, Georgia's First Printer
By Alexander A. Lawrence. Savannah, Georgia, 1956.
Designed and decorated with linocuts by Ray Dilley.

Catalogue for a book exhibition
set in Linotype Pilgrim

32 line mechanical composition

Linotype and Intertype machines, producing type in slug form, are mainly installed in newspapers but are also to be found in many book and general printers. Designers of print seem chary of specifying line composition, partly because it is less commonly available for general jobbing, but perhaps also from lack of knowledge of the machines' capabilities. In certain classes of work this system of typesetting offers economic advantages and relative freedom from constrictions on the design.

In the first place changes of type face and size, provided these are not too many, are perfectly economic, even when only a few lines of each are required. Again, the number of alphabets available for setting in the same line need not be limited to seven, depending on the model of machine and the printer's stock of types. Change of measure poses no more problems than it does with Monotype, but the maximum is 30 ems, above which lines must be set in two sections, with some possible ill effect to word spacing.

An objection sometimes levelled at line composition is the quality of the printed image obtained from it. This should not be distinguishable from single-type quality except when the stock is coated, and even then if the composing machine is in good condition and care is exercised in the printing, the result should be quite satisfactory.

Greater limits are set to the design of typefaces for line composing, producing aesthetically less pleasing letterforms in some instances. The impossibility of 'kerned' letters leads to excessively wide spaced italic in many founts and to a few distorted characters, notably lowercase *f*. In order to make use of duplex matrices, roman, italic and bold are usually of the same alphabet length. These restrictions inevitably affect the appearance of line-set work to some extent.

Letterspacing is not an economic proposition, but may occasionally be asked for in the largest sizes, though the niceties of visual letterspacing are impractical.

Calculations of the area occupied by a certain amount of copy when set in the chosen fount to a given measure are made in the same way as for Monotype, this time using the tables supplied by the Linotype and Intertype companies. As with single-type composition, lines can be cast on a larger body size to obviate leading. There are no set-width complications in line composing, but restrictions are placed on tabular setting, as can be learned in the next section.

A selection of rules, borders, ornaments and sorts is available and line composition can be supplemented by the products, in slug form, of the Ludlow or similar machine. Hand setting can of course also be specified when particularly desired for reason of typeface, but one of the economic advantages of the system is that mechanical means can be employed through-out.

Reference to the printer's list of types and sizes available or to his type-book if he has one is essential before beginning a layout.

Prepare a working layout for an announcement to be inserted in a trade monthly magazine, printed black only on SC newsprint. Setting is entirely by Linotype/Intertype, the maximum type area is 30 ems deep by 15 ems, and copy is as follows: 'Introductory Map Reading/Topo-graphical maps in world-wide sample studies/I. C. Marshall, M.A. and A. H. Heux, M.A./*700 characters text*/ Publishing October 26/University of London Press Limited/St Paul's House, Warwick Lane, London E4C 2PB'.

102

Extract from
the *Radio Times*
set in Intertype Royal
*reproduced by permission
of the Radio Times*

BBC2　　　　**21 November Friday** *tv*

11.0 am *Colour*
Play School
Science Day
Today's story is 'What a Crop'
by JOANNE COLE
Presenters
MIRANDA CONNELL, LIONEL MORTON
Pianist JONATHAN COHEN
Scripted and directed by MICHAEL COLE
Series producer CYNTHIA FELGATE †
(repeated on BBC1 and BBC Wales at
4.20 pm)

11.20 Closedown

7.0
What are the Facts –
about Antibiotics?
Scientists produce antibiotics –
microbes develop resistance. How
long can we keep one step ahead?
An enquiry by DEREK COOPER with
DR E. S. ANDERSON, FRS
G. C. BRANDER, MRCVS
DR M J LEWIS
DR H. WILLIAMS SMITH
A CONSULTANT PHYSICIAN
Directed by FRANCIS FUCHS
Produced by EURFRON GWYNNE JONES †

7.30 *Colour*
Newsroom
Reporting the world tonight
JOHN TIMPSON and PETER WOODS
and **Weather**

8.0 *Colour*
Wheelbase
The Rally of the Forests
GORDON WILKINS covers the world
of motoring
The top event in the British rally
calendar, the RAC, ended on Wed-
nesday night in London after a
five-day battle between some of
the best competition drivers in the
world. British Leyland and Ford
entered Andrew Cowan, Roger
Clark and Paddy Hopkirk against
the fastest of the 'Flying Finns'
Rauno Aaltonen, Timo Makinen
and Hannu Mikkola. The 2,500-
mile rally route went through the
mountains of North Wales, the
Lake District, and the lowlands
of Scotland, including 60 flat-out
speed tests over forest tracks.
Directors CHRIS BERRY, TONY SALMON
Associate producers JOHN MILLS,
CHRISTOPHER RAINBOW
Producer BRIAN ROBINS

8.25 *Colour*
The First Churchills
by DONALD WILSON
(shown on Saturday)

9.10
The French Cinema
Trois Chambres à
Manhattan
(*Three Rooms in Manhattan*)
starring
Annie Girardot, Maurice Ronet
with
O. E. Hasse, Genevieve Page
Two young French people, an
actor and a divorcee, alone in
New York, gradually reveal their
problems and uncertainties and
find happiness together.
Marcel Carné, the director of the
classic *Les Enfants du Paradis*,
and his cameraman Eugen Shuftan have successfully captured
the oppressive atmosphere of New
York in this moving love story,
starring two of France's leading
actors, Maurice Ronet and Annie
Girardot.

Kay.................ANNIE GIRARDOT
François.............MAURICE RONET
Hourvitch...............O. E. HASSE
Yolande..........GENEVIEVE PAGE
Pierre..........ROLAND LESAFFRE
Comte Larsi....GABRIELE FERZETTI
Photographed by EUGEN SHUFTAN
Screenplay by MARCEL CARNÉ
and JACQUES SIGURD
Based on the novel of GEORGES SIMENON
Directed by MARCEL CARNÉ
Produced by PHILIPPE SENNE

10.55 *Colour*
Westminster at Work
David Holmes looks back over
the past week in Parliament and
introduces reports and big de-
bates in both Houses, questions
to Ministers, significant moves behind the scenes, and the effects
of MPs' work inside and outside
Westminster
Editor JOHN DANVERS

11.15 *Colour*
News Summary
and **Weather**

11.20 *Colour*
Line-up: Friday
Talk, argument, people, diversion
Editor ROWAN AYERS

33 tables without rules

Certain information is most clearly and succinctly conveyed by means of tabular setting. On the other hand, such treatment is occasionally accorded to copy which would be more readily understood if put into simple sentences, and these the typographer should bring to the notice of the author. Even more efficient ways of presenting complex information of a certain nature are possible if graphic techniques are adopted: for example, the histogram and the graph, but these are properly outside the scope of this book.

The logic implied in spacing was discussed early in the book. The placing of words on the page in positions which demonstrate their relationship to one another is also the principle behind tabular setting. Type set in ranged columns can be considered as an extended application of the grouping principle:

The first figure is a simple treatment of a list with two columns, each item explained by its position as one of a vertical column of similar items and also having a visible connection with the wording with which it shares a line horizontally. In this way a visual cross-reference is established through the

Reverse of card
for Clydesdale Bank

Clydesdale Bank Limited

Head Office	PO Box No 43 30 St Vincent Place Glasgow C1

	We can help you with your
TRAVEL REQUIREMENTS	by the issue of Letters of Credit, Travellers Cheques and Foreign Money
STOCKS AND SHARES	by buying and selling on your instructions
GIFT PROBLEMS	by the issue of our Gift Cheques for special occasions
WILL OR SETTLEMENT	through our Executor and Trustee Department
LOANS	by way of Overdraft or Personal Loan
INVESTMENT PORTFOLIO SUPERVISION	through our Investment Management Service

Your Branch Manager will be glad to explain these and other services to you method of setting. The treatment shown in the second figure loses read-ability when the left-hand column has too many words per line. In the last figure a common alternative is demonstrated. The unsightly practice of inserting dotted lines (leaders) should be avoided, unless the gap between left and right columns is so great and interlinear space so scarce that the eye is otherwise incapable of relating the two.

Only the first arrangement can be applied to three or more columns, and the vertical and horizontal groupings are often made explicit by the addition of headings above and/or before the main matter:

104

Society of Typographic Designers programme of lectures 1964/1965

all lectures commence at 6.30 pm
at the National Book League, 7 Albemarle St, W1

5 November	**Looking and thinking** Frank Overton, design consultant
30 November	**Photography for advertising** Bob Brooks, photographer
7 January	**Talk on graphics** Robert Brownjohn, graphic designer, art director
4 February	**'A conversation'** Germano Facetti, art director, Penguin Books Ltd
4 March	**Figure brand image archetype** Edward Wright, teacher, designer
1 April	**The IBM corporate image** R G Smith, advertising director, IBM, UK
6 May	**New thinking with Letraset** Fred Lambert, designer, typographer
3 June	**Annual General Meeting**

Programme printed violet and brown
for Society of Typographic Designers

Pages from a brochure
for DALTA
printed black and purple

Tabular matter is machine-set and comparison of the two main methods of composition reveals that the accurate ranging of words or lines at points within the line (multi-justification) is possible only with Monotype. With line-set type, each column has to be set separately and the whole table assembled afterwards. In the previous figure, Monotype could set straight across in one measure, but line composing would set each column separately, five measures in all. This is a decided disadvantage in complex work.

When designing tables without rules for Monotype, each sub-measure within the line should as far as possible be even ems o/b, not in 12pt ems. As seen in section 31, the set of the type must be known, since it determines the width of the em-quad. Though most typographers leave the precise calculation of the column widths to the operator, it is sometimes necessary to know what is involved before an accurate layout is at all possible. Monotype Corporation issue a combination set-em scale with the various set-width scales on it, indispensable to the accurate drawing-up of this kind of work. In the case of line composition, all measures, being independent, are in 12pt ems.

Page from *Wine Mine*
published by Peter Dominic

Gin

GIN

Strengths are 70° proof unless otherwise indicated.

Item		½ gal	bot	½ bot	¼ bot	min
1601	**Dominic' Finest London Dry** 65°	143/-	49/11	25/9		
	Excellent gin for cocktails; purchase in half-gallon jars saves 2s 3d a bottle.					
1617	**Foster's Military**		52/9	27/3		
1602	**Gilbey's London Dry**		52/9	27/3	14/-	
1605	**Burnett's** White Satin		52/9	27/3	14/-	
1603	**Booth's** Finest London Dry		52/9	27/3	14/-	5/3
1604	**Booth's High & Dry**		52/9	27/3		
1606	**Gordon's** Special Dry London		52/9	27/3	14/-	5/3
1607	**Plymouth** Coate's original		53/-	27/4		
1608	**Beefeater Extra Dry** pure grain		52/9	27/3		
1609	**Gordon's Old Tom** (sweetened)		52/9			
1610	**Holland's Gin** Bols Geneve 66°		57/8	29/6		
1611	**Holland's Gin** de Kuyper's 69°		57/-	29/3		
1612	**Steinhager** Echter 66.4° Stone Cruchon		55/6			

GIN CORDIALS

Item		bot	½ bot
1620	**Bessen Coeburgh's Blackcurrant** Geneva 40°	40/-	
1623	**Hawker's Pedlar Sloe** 45°	46/3	23/9

BITTERS

Bitters are spirits containing a concentrated infusion of aromatic herbs, fruit peels and stones and used for flavouring gin and cocktails.

Item		bot	½ bot	min
1653	**Angostura** 78°		29/9	9/1
1651	**Law's Peach** 15°	20/6	10/9	
1659	**Gordon's Orange** 41°	35/9		
1654	**Amer Picon** 46°	49/-		
1656	**Fernet Branca** 78°	78/-	40/3	3/9
1657	**Ferro China** Bisleri 34°	46/-		
1658	**Amaro 18** Isolabella 56°	57/-		
1662	**Underberg** 86°			3/6
1660	**Finsbury Orange**	20/6		

Here is a typical entry in an exhibition catalogue. Make an accurate and fully-marked-up layout showing the tabular style to be adopted in setting by (a) Monotype and (b) Linotype or Intertype, to a measure of 24 ems. Columns are separated in the following copy by the solidus/: '141/Carlo Levi/Portrait of the poet Pablo Neruda/1936/Oil on canvas/ $28\frac{3}{4}\times 36\frac{1}{4}$in'.

First choose a legible typeface and a likely size. Decide on alphabets and accurately cast-off the widths of the various columns, based on the longest line in each. This is at the discretion of the typographer, who is at liberty to turn words over into the next line. In the case of Monotype remember that column measures should be in even ems o/b, with the exception of one which will contain a fraction of an em to make up exactly the total 24 em measure. Adequate space, more than one em o/b, must separate columns visually. Set in a small type size or turn lines over rather than crowd columns together.

Tabular matter lends itself admirably to asymmetric design, since it is itself a grid made up of ranged lines. Its vertical axis may be shared with accompanying display matter, thus:

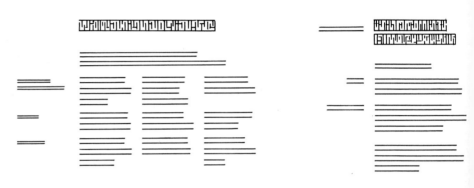

Design a contents/title page for a magazine, trimmed size 215×140mm ($8\frac{1}{2}\times5\frac{1}{2}$in), type area 42 ems $\times26$ ems, printed in black and light blue on coated stock. Bleed is possible if desired. The typeface used on the text pages is 10/11pt Monotype Plantin series 110 and this fount should be used for the bulk of the typesetting. The copy is:

'Teen/A magazine of current events and ideas for the under-twenty-ones/ January 19xx/Volume 1/Number 1/ Editor: James McGee/Published by Kegan and Paul Routledge Ltd, Museum Street, London W1A 7RR. Contents
Design today/New materials, ideas and techniques in chairs, bicycles and transistors/A. E. Chisholm/page 4
The folk music revival/Old songs and a new treatment/Joan Dillon/page 8
Guarantees/What are they worth?/ R. S. Mooney/page 10
Emigration/Who goes where and why?/L. Tyson/page 12
New paperbacks/page 14
Letters to the editor/page 15'.

34 tables with rules

In accordance with the principle of economy of means, which earlier led us to eliminate inessential punctuation, tables without rules are to be preferred to tables with rules, unless reference is made easier for the reader by their inclusion. This happens in complex tabular settings and where insufficient space is available to separate items from each other.

The undesirable effect of too many straight lines seen at once has already been stressed. This and a contemporary fashion for simplicity must lead us to use only the absolute minimum of rules required to make sense of the wording. In a table having headings top and side the minimum will be two, as in fig. 1, but in some cases it may be useful to add top and bottom rules to separate the table from accompanying text, as in fig. 2. Additional down rules, and more rarely cross rules, are introduced only when confusion would otherwise result. Then the added rules should be finer than the main ones, as shown in fig. 3. Boxed tables, completely enclosed by rules, are only now and then unavoidable.

The calculation of column measures in tables is complicated by the vertical rules, whose width must be allowed for. Monotype still sets across the total measure, including a throw-away space at the end of the line, equal to the combined widths of the vertical rules, which can then be inserted. Various body widths of rule exist to choose from, a short list appearing in section 14. Again, although in many settings the operator will carry out all necessary calculations and adjustments, in complex tabular work a knowledge of what is involved helps greatly in its preparation.

To give an example, if fig. 3 were to be set in Monotype $8\frac{1}{2}$ set, a preliminary cast-off of the column widths might be: 12, 10, 10, 11 and 12 ems, equalling 55 ems o/b, that is, about 470 pts. The total measure, let us say, is 24 ems or 480 pts. A 2pt full-face and three 2pt fine rules are asked for, totalling 8 in pts. This makes a total width of 478 pts, leaving a small amount of space to be added by the operator to whichever column he thinks fit.

Column measures need not be written on the layout, but their accurate drawing helps in the setting and enables the typographer to specify particular widths of rule with confidence.

There are two distinct methods of adding cross rules in a table. Either continuous rules may be cut and inserted by hand, or a series of em-dashes, which print as an unbroken line, can be set by machine. When em-dashes are used, all columns must be in even ems of the set of the fount, unless en-dashes are available. Whenever vertical and horizontal lines cross each other frequently in a table, the em-dash method of providing cross-rules saves laborious and expensive cutting of rule by hand.

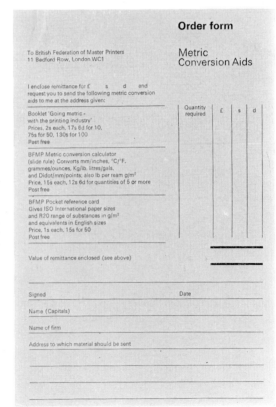

Order form
for British Federation
of Master Printers

Order form

To British Federation of Master Printers
11 Bedford Row, London WC1

Metric
Conversion Aids

I enclose remittance for £   s   d   and
request you to send the following metric conversion
aids to me at the address given:

Booklet 'Going metric -
with the printing industry'
Prices, 2s each, 17s 6d for 10,
75s for 50, 130s for 100
Post free

BFMP Metric conversion calculator
(slide rule) Converts mm/inches, °C/°F,
grammes/ounces, Kg/lb, litres/gals,
and Didot/mm/points; also lb per ream g/m²
Price, 15s each, 12s 6d for quantities of 5 or more
Post free

BFMP Pocket reference card
Gives ISO International paper sizes
and R20 range of substances in g/m²
and equivalents in English sizes
Price, 1s each, 15s for 50
Post free

Quantity
required   £   s   d

Value of remittance enclosed (see above)

Signed   Date

Name (Capitals)

Name of firm

Address to which material should be sent

In all tables accurate joins between rules are difficult to obtain.

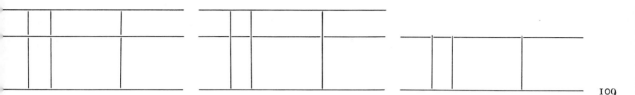

The first diagram represents a table where the down rules have been cut to allow the cross rules to remain intact. Unless full-face rule is used, the gap between is always apparent, but is optically less obvious when the procedure is reversed and the cross rules cut, as in the next figure. Lines of em-dashes machine-set are identical to this in effect, but top and bottom rules should always be continuous, to avoid the effect represented in the final figure at the top.

Perfect joins between lines meeting or crossing are ensured only by adopting one of the following courses. Down and cross rules can be set and printed separately, one on top of the other. As this doubles the amount of printing to be done, when the run is large the method is prohibitively expensive. If however a second colour is already available, the table may be so designed that down rules are in one colour, cross rules in the other, thus incurring no extra expense.

As an alternative, the lines of the table can be drawn in indian ink on bristol board, perfect type pulls pasted in position, and a plate made of the whole. The cost of the plate must be considered.

Like tabular matter, tables with rules fit in well with asymmetric layouts. Items consisting of a number of lines of copy are better ranged left and along the top, and side headings are often better ranged to the right, as in fig. 1. In this figure too, a vertical axis has been created by the use of a bold rule.

Problems peculiar to particular copy can be solved by application of the principles learned here. For example, a suitable answer to a difficulty arising from too long headings and short items, combined with a narrow overall measure, might be as suggested below:

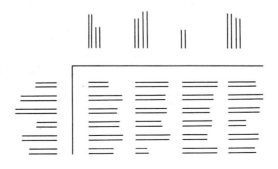

Prepare a working layout for a table with rules set to a measure of 24 ems in 10pt type throughout, face optional, and to be printed in black and one colour. The copy has been received in this form:

110

PRICE LIST.

No.	Artist.	Title.	U.K. Price.	U.S. Price.
1.	Prunella Clough.	Tideline.	12 gns.	$40
2.	Alan Davie.	Sleeping Angel.	15 gns.	$50
3.	Josef Herman.	Mother and child.	15 gns.	$50
4.	John Piper.	Beach in Brittany.	20 gns.	$65

Besides superfluous punctuation, in much tabular work there are also unnecessary words. The heading 'No.' and the words 'price' are surely redundant. The repetitions of 'gns' and the dollar sign can be avoided by altering the respective headings to 'UK gns' and 'US $' or even simply 'gns' and '$', if no ambiguity would arise. All of the punctuation marks can be deleted from the copy.

Column widths will be decided by the desirability of the longest line in each fitting comfortably into it, without crowding or excessive space. The alphabets chosen will also influence them. Variation of alphabet, particularly between heading and the body of the table, helps the reader's understanding. If the student feels that one column deserves more emphasis than the other, an alphabet change for that column gives it the desired importance. Roman capitals with lowercase, being the most legible, are of course employed for the bulk of the reading matter.

DALTA booking form
printed red and black

Booking Form   **DALTA Season**

Box Office Manager
King's Theatre Glasgow
telephone City 5125-7

Please exercise extreme care when completing this form to ensure that dates, production titles, prices and parts of theatre correspond

Mistakes may delay delivery of your tickets

Cheques, postal and money orders etc to be crossed and made payable to the Corporation of Glasgow

Production	Evening/ Matinée	Part of Theatre	Date	Alternative Date	No. of Tickets	Price

Dalta Special Concession
For every combined ticket purchased for the following five performances (21 September, 5, 16, 27 October, 9 November) **one** *free* guest ticket will be given for each of the five performances listed

No of combined tickets	Part of Theatre	Price

Name

Address

Telephone

I enclose stamped, addressed envelope and Postal Order/cheque for

The availability of a second colour prompts some observations. The printing of all down rules in colour means that no allowance has to be made for their widths in setting the type, because these rules are imposed in a separate forme. Also, as already pointed out, if all the rules in one direction are in a different colour from those in the other direction, joins are perfect and make-up simplified. But avoid the case where a rule in one colour touches without crossing one in another colour, as this raises register problems in make-up and on the press. Revise sections 17 to 19 on the use of colour before continuing with the exercise.

When the above decisions have been taken, cast-off roughly the length of the longest line in each column. Then add approximately equal amounts to each column in order to make up to the full 24 em measure. Wherever possible, bring each sub measure to even ems o/b. Down rules in black take up space and have to be included in the calculation. Mark-up the layout fully in the usual way.

Pages from Swissair timetable
printed red and black

Destination	Frequency	FROM LONDON Departure	Arrival	Flight No.	Aircraft	Frequency	TO LONDON Departure	Arrival	Flight No.	Aircraft	Class	FARES UK £ Single	Return
RIO DE JANEIRO Galeão	Th	1950	a*0845	SR 807/SR 200	D9/D8	Tu	a0135	1910	SR 201/SR 812	D8/D9	Y	170.17	324.12
	Su	1950	a*0925	SR 807/SR 202	D9/D8	Sa	a0135	1910	SR 203/SR 812	D8/D9	F	305. 0	579.10
ROME Fiumicino	Daily	1015	1540	SR 801/AZ 401	D9	Daily	0945	1340	SR 611/BE 555	D9/HT	Y	38. 5	72.14
	Daily	1120	1550	SR 811/AZ 411	CA	Daily	1220	1910	AZ 410/SR 812	CA/D9	F	53.17	102. 7
	Daily	1525	1950	SR 813/SR 612	D9	Mo Th 23/12–6/3	2020	*0030	SR 609/BE 573	D9/HT			
						Fr Sa 20/12–31/3	2020	*0030	SR 609/BE 573	D9/HT			
SANTIAGO Pudahuel	Th	1950	*1420	SR 807/SR 200	D9/D8	Mo	1630	*1910	SR 201/SR 812	D8/D9	Y	211.14	402. 4
	Su	1950	*1500	SR 807/SR 202	D9/D8	Fr	1630	*1910	SR 203/SR 812	D8/D9	F	343.15	653. 3
SAO PAULO Viracopos	Th	1950	a*1030	SR 807/SR 200	D9/D8	Mo	a2355	*1910	SR 201/SR 812	D8/D9	Y	175. 0	332.10
	Su	1950	a*1110	SR 807/SR 202	D9/D8	Fr	a2355	*1910	SR 203/SR 812	D8/D9	F	309.12	588. 4
TEHERAN	We	1015	2240	SR 801/SR 374	D9/C9	Tu Sa	1050	1910	SR 373/SR 812	C9/D9	Y	120. 4	228. 8
	Fr	1120	2245	SR 811/SR 372	CA/C9	Th	1050	1910	SR 375/SR 812	C9/D9	Y		f153.18
	Mo	1120	2245	SR 811/SR 370	CA/C9						F	173.17	330. 7
TEL AVIV	Mo Tu Th	1015	1735	SR 801/SR 330	D9/C9	Mo Tu We Fr	0735	1300	SR 331/BE 565	C9/HT	Y	87.11	166. 7
	We	0925	1800	BE 564/SR 334	HT/C9	Th	0735	1435	SR 335/SR 804	C9/D9	Y		f112. 2
	Su	1120	1835	SR 811/SR 338	CA/C9	Su	1335	1910	SR 333/SR 812	D8/D9	F	129.11	246. 3
	Sa 14/12–31/3	2315	*1230	SR 861/SR 332	D9/D8								
TOKYO	Mo	1015	*2045	SR 801/SK 983	D9/D8	Tu	1100	*0920	SR 305/SR 800	C9/D9	Y	282. 7	536.10
	Th	1015	*2155	SR 801/SK 985	D9/D8	Th	1130	*0920	SR 301/SR 800	C9/D9	F	469. 1	891. 4
	Su	1015	*2015	SR 801/SR 304	D9/C9	Fr	1130	*0920	SR 307/SR 800	C9/D9			
	Tu	1120	*2115	SR 811/SR 300	CA/C9	Su	1130	*0920	SR 303/SR 800	C9/D9			
	We	1120	*1950	SR 811/SR 306	CA/C9	We	1215	*0920	SK 984/SR 800	D8/D9			
	Fr	1120	*2015	SR 811/SR 302	CA/C9	Sa	1215	*0920	SK 986/SR 800	D8/D9			
TRIPOLI	Th	1120	1815	SR 811/SR 240	CA/C9	Fr	0815	1340	SR 241/BE 555	C9/HT	Y	46. 7	88. 2
											F	68.10	130. 3
TUNIS	Su	1020	1450	BE 554/SR 244	HT/CA	Fr	0900	1340	SR 241/BE 555	C9/HT	Y	39.17	75.15
	Mo	1120	1740	SR 811/TU 903	CA	Su	1535	2015	SR 245/BE 559	CA/HT	Y		f68.17
	Th	1120	1530	SR 811/SR 240	CA/C9						F	50. 3	95. 6
	Sa	1120	1730	SR 811/TU 901	CA								

Explanation of symbols and abbreviations see page 24

Copy for a booklet
typed and fully marked-up
for mechanical composition

Page 1

1/ OPENING REMARKS/

The Chairman constituted conference.

Mr/ Blakey as Host Principal welcomed members.

Mr/ Gray: In proposing the conference, Chamber had made two assumptions:

(i) Principals had right to receive fuller information without which they might become too detached from day-to-day industry.

(ii) Chamber would welcome chance to know more of what the Colleges could offer.

2/ DO CHANGES IN MODERN OFFICE TECHNIQUES DEMAND A REVIEW OF COMMERCIAL TRAINING?

The Chairman raised questions on teaching of purchasing, cost reduction techniques, costing, machine accounting, production control, data processing and purchasing techniques.

Mr/ Ebbage suggested 3 types of possible courses:-

(i) Afternoon background courses for senior management (half lecture and half discussion);

(ii) Terminal courses for executives; and

(iii) Longer courses for clerical staffs.

Mr/ Gray pled for juniors to have more training in these techniques.

Mr/ Forbes MacPherson said that industry was becoming more alive to the need for specialists. E.g., there was a shortage of programmers for computers. Here indeed was an opening for the new type of clever office-boy (-) to train for H/N/C/ and specialize in computers. In U/S/A/, such were recruited from Colleges, but such workers had to accept shift-working conditions, for such machines had to be kept going 24 hours a day. These new techniques were fashionable but costly and

/tended

So far, we have been concerned only with a single sheet of paper, printed one 113
side. The time has come to attempt work running to several pages, as in a
booklet or book. We shall not deal with the traditionally designed book,
which is well treated elsewhere, most comprehensively in Williamson:
Methods of book design and Lee: *Bookmaking*. The design of booklets, on the
other hand, is not much written about and it is with this that we will deal now.

In printing as in other industries, standardization effects useful economies.
Multi-page work should as far as practicable have its pages designed to a
standard layout, particularly as regards overall width and depth, but also in
respect of typefaces and sizes, measures and spacing. Even when only a single
line of type appears on a page of a booklet, the compositor makes up this page
to the same dimensions as the other pages in the job, by blanking out with
spacing material. Standardization of the basic elements of the page greatly
facilitates setting, make-up, imposition and machining.

Similarity of treatment between all the pages of a job is also desirable
from an aesthetic viewpoint, as it is important to the unity of the overall
design. Except in more complex work, it is possible to convey all the instructions governing the general layout of text pages in a booklet by drawing up
one specimen double spread and marking up the typescript for details of
variations within this style.

For economic reasons, as many pages as possible are printed simultaneously, subject to limitations of sheet and machine sizes. The common

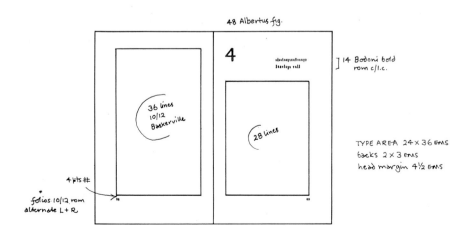

impositions are of 4, 8 and 16 pages in a forme and the total number of pages in a job is in multiples and sums of these. For instance, a 48-page booklet would quite likely be printed in three 16-page sections, while a 36-page booklet would for preference be made up of one 4-page and two 16-page sections. The fewer sections there are, the less time it takes to impose, print and bind. On occasion, when the run is short, it may cost no more to produce 16 pages than it would to print 12 (8 and 4), owing to savings in production time. See Garland: *Graphics Handbook* for some typical imposition schemes.

Do not make the beginner's mistake of designing the cover before the inside pages, though it may appear to offer the more attractive assignment. As will be seen, the requirements of the text pages affect its layout.

When a booklet is opened, what is actually viewed is not two independent pages but a single sheet folded down the middle. A beginning can therefore be made by drawing this double spread lightly on the layout paper, indicating the fold by another line. The dimensions should be a standard sub-division of an available stock, handy for the pocket. When printed and folded, the booklet has to be trimmed on three sides to free the pages: at head, tail and foredge. Draw a firm line representing the trimmed size, 3mm ($\frac{1}{8}$in) inside the area already drawn. If it is intended to bleed at any edge of any page, 6mm ($\frac{1}{4}$in) trim all round is recommended. This gives the largest possible finished dimensions from the selected standard paper size, but should for any reason a slightly smaller format be wanted, no difficulty arises.

114

Prepare working layouts for a pocket booklet entitled 'Photoengraving/A beginner's guide'. This title should appear on the cover. Copy for the text consists of 11 pages of typescript, each having 40 lines with an average of 60 character/spaces per line. One paper is to be used throughout and printing is in black only.

Bleed or exceptionally narrow margins, combined with minimum trim, can sometimes present problems when they occur at the grip edge of the sheet. With the larger sheet sizes being dealt with in this kind of work, the grip i always at one of the longer sides of the full sheet. If there is the slightest chance of difficulties arising on this score, consult the printer, who will carry out his own check and may be able to alter his imposition if necessary. He will say if a smaller finished size is advisable.

The area of print on each page has next to be decided. Length of measure depends on typeface, size and leading, also on whether the text is to be accommodated in few or many pages. Only a provisional decision has to be made at this stage.

As regards margins, work with up to 8 pages and sometimes beyond can be treated in a manner similar to leaflets: equal space on three sides, extra at the foot, as in fig. 1. In jobs extending to 16 or more pages it is suggested that book practice be followed and the unity of the double spread be recognized by positioning the type areas as in fig. 2. The three margins formed by the foredges and the combined backs should appear equal, though due to the optical effect of the fold it is necessary to increase the backs at the expense of the foredges to achieve this. The head margin looks best if rather less than a foredge, while the tail margin is, as before, greater than any other.

A deeper understanding of such margins can be gained from Williamson: *Methods of Book design*. In the final resort the eye alone must be the judge as to whether a satisfactory relationship has been found between paper and text areas. The eye can be trained only by intelligent study of the work of the best typographers, past and present.

Folios (page numbers) are only desirable in those cases where use can be made of them by the reader, otherwise they should be omitted. If included, the folio should appear above or below the text, towards the foredge for easy reference, and outside the type area established, so that it does not affect its proportions. Figures are always better than roman numerals or words. The arrangement shown in fig. 4 is sound but involves more intricate page-make-up which may prove expensive if many pages are involved. Running head-lines should not be used in booklets unless some way is found of making them of direct value to the reader.

116

It remains to choose a typeface of readable size, related to reading distance but also influenced by the size of the page, and suitably leaded if wanted. From mechanical composition copyfitting tables work out the number of character/spaces contained in one page of your layout. As the total character count is given in the exercise, the number of pages of text the job will make if set to the projected type area and style can be simply calculated.

It can now be seen whether, allowing for a cover page, the booklet as designed will make a number of pages which suits the requirements of pro-duction referred to earlier. It is preferable, if not essential, to leave the reverse of the cover blank, especially if the paper is less than opaque. The last page too is often better left unprinted, particularly so in this instance as text there might in time become obscured through wear in the pocket. If too many additional blank pages are needed to complete the total, it is better to reduce or increase the character content of the page by adjusting the type area, type size or leading, until the amount of type and the available pages coincide to a more reasonable degree.

A final layout of the double spread can now be attempted, with backs and heads marked in ems and details of measure, typeface, size, leading and number of lines per page marked up. In practice, this layout would be accompanied by the typescript, fully marked up for style as laid down in section 31.

Now proceed with the cover layout. Inside the trimmed size draw the margins appropriate to a right-hand text page. The typeface and style of setting must closely conform to those of the text pages. Finally, specify the paper according to the criteria of section 28, paying attention to suitability of typeface to paper surface, and write down a numbered list of all the pages in the booklet, noting against each whether 'cover', 'text' or 'blank', as a guide to the printer.

Pages from *Monotype Recorder*
devoted to Stanley Morison

Prepare working layouts and give full instructions for the production of the following booklet:
Cover, to be separate: 'Training for skill/Recruitment and training of young workers in industry/Report by a sub-committee of the National Joint Advisory Council/published for the Ministry of Labour by Her Majesty's Stationery Office/Price 15p net'.
Title page: 'Training for skill/Recruitment and training of young workers in industry/Report by a sub-committee of the National Joint Advisory Council/ London/Her Majesty's Stationery Office'.
Contents: 'Contents' followed by 23 items, the longest of which reads: '12. Graduate, student and technician apprentices', page reference being given in every case.
Preface: 'Preface' with text amounting to 1380 character/spaces.
Text: typescript consisting of 34 pages, averaging 2150 character/spaces each. The text is divided into 23 sections of equal importance, the wording for the longest being '12. Graduate, student and technician apprentices'.

The aim of the designer of multi-page work is, first, to attract attention and create interest in the contents by means of the cover; then to inform without fuss but in a manner which sustains interest through the preliminary pages; lastly, to make readable the body of the text without distractions.

The nature of the booklet form, where the total design concept is never seen as a whole at any one moment, but is revealed in stages as the pages are turned, borders on the cinematographic. Logical gradation of emphasis, unity of style and dramatic effect from spread to spread must all be considered by the designer.

In this more ambitious project the cover is to be printed separately from the text and on a different stock. The material selected must be appreciably stronger than the text paper envisaged, otherwise the cheaper method of 'own paper' cover as used in the previous exercise would suffice. The weight and strength of the cover stock will also depend on the bulk of the combined inside pages. If both cover and text papers are white, check that their whiteness is identical, otherwise show a decided change of colour between them. As the two materials are not necessarily available in the same standard sheet size, make sure that a size for the finished booklet is settled which comes economically out of both.

The text matter in this exercise is divided into sections. The space occupied by the 23 displayed headings must be estimated and taken into account when working out the total number of pages in the job. A working layout for a specimen double spread, marked up as before, but including a layout for a section heading which acts as a model for all the others, can again be drawn. The stipulation is for 'run-on' headings, that is, sections are to follow on the same page as the end of the preceding section after a short space, and are not each to begin at the top of a fresh page. As a list of contents is included in the booklet, folios are obligatory.

The precise function of the cover must be understood. In this exercise it is primarily informative, rather than eye-catching, and the certain dignity proper to official publications precludes more dramatic treatment. Try to attain a certain liveliness without losing sight of the nature of the content. A second colour may be used.

The title page must be similar in style to the cover but cannot be a mere repeat of it, since it is not meant to be read at arm's length nor should it seem to attract attention to itself. Therefore it will be less emphatic and make use of smaller type sizes, though face and alphabets will probably match those on the cover. Layouts for cover and title page should now be made, sketching roughs for both before attempting full-size working layouts. Black ink only may be used on inside pages.

The contents page may appear on the reverse of the title, with the first text page opposite, but unless dictated by economy this is not advised because of its cheap and crowded look. If contents and the opening page of the text both occupy right-hand positions, the pauses occasioned by the intervening blanks give the reader a pleasant sense of space and leisure. This page is really a list, so revise section 33 before beginning its layout.

A working layout for the first page of the preface is also needed. Style is identical to the text pages and, as in the contents, the same type size as the text may be specified, though the entire preface may be set in italics if desired, to differentiate it from the main text.

Finally, list as before the pages in the job, writing 'title', 'blank', 'text' and so on after each folio, as before. Add full details of papers, inks and mechanical composition.

It is customary in this kind of work to ask for a set of galley proofs of the type before make-up but after reader's corrections have been made, for pasting up into a dummy copy. This greatly helps the compositor in making up pages and allows the typographer to sort out any difficulties in advance. Take careful note that this use of galley proofs certainly does not mean that casting-off type and deciding on number of pages can be left until the dummy is being prepared. The job must be planned in every detail *before* setting.

Title page and double spread
of a booklet
for the Department of Fine Art
University of Glasgow

W. A. CARGILL
MEMORIAL LECTURES
IN FINE ART

I

Patronage and
Prejudice

T. J. HONEYMAN

UNIVERSITY OF GLASGOW
1968

When a printed job consists of more than one sheet of paper, some means of holding the separate sheets together has to be found. As there is more than one way of doing this, and as the method used has a bearing on the design of the work, some knowledge of binding methods is of value to the typographer.

In the previous two examples it was tacitly assumed that the common saddle-back style of binding was to be adopted. As demonstrated below, such a booklet is open in the middle and a sufficient number of wire staples inserted through the back. This is cheap and convenient but hardly strong enough for work likely to receive continual handling and expected to last a long time, particularly if the paper is rather weak. Thread may be used to give a little more permanence but it is more costly. A further disadvantage is that the wires are visible on the outside of the cover. Most important, there is a limit to the number of pages which can safely be secured by the saddle-back method, and as the job becomes bulkier there is an increasing tendency for the pages to refuse to lie flat when shut, as represented in the diagram under:

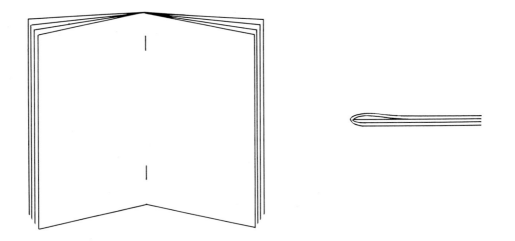

The common alternatives in such a case are side-stitching or stabbing. By either method each complete section of pages is folded and laid on top of the last, the whole being joined together by staples driven through the back margin, as illustrated under. A separate cover is essential to conceal the wires and this is glued to the spine and also over the staples. With heavy papers it is advisable to crease at the points indicated by arrows:

A square back is formed by this style of binding and therefore a spine must be included in the design for the cover. Its width is found by measuring that of a dummy copy of the booklet made up of the correct number of pages of the paper for the job.

Opening the pages of a booklet bound in this way is less convenient to the reader than is the case with other methods, because pages will not lie open by themselves. The cover is liable to come apart, too, but otherwise a very strong binding is created. When making margins, an extra 9mm ($\frac{3}{4}$in) must be added to the back margin of every page because of the space occupied by the wires and the difficulty of opening the pages fully.

With stabbed work impositions are radically different from saddle-stitched. As can be deducted from comparison of the diagrams, in the case of saddle-back each sheet and section of sheets gets half its pages from the front and half from the rear of the job. On the other hand, each section in stabbed work consists of consecutively numbered pages.

This fact is economically important when a limited amount of colour printing is proposed. By studying the printer's scheme of imposition a design can be produced which confines colour to a few sections only in a booklet, without this economy being too apparent to the reader. When contrasting kinds of paper are to be used together within the text pages, a knowledge of the imposition intended by the printer is again vital to determining their placing.

Another way of unobtrusively limiting additional workings is to specify the second colour on one side of the paper only. When a section treated so is folded and trimmed, the colour is seen on alternate double spreads. This is feasible only when the work is being printed sheetwork, that is, a type forme for each side of the sheet. The other possibility is halfsheetwork, where all the pages in the section, whether printing on the front or back of the paper, are included in one forme. The paper is cut twice as large, printed, turned over and reprinted from the same type so that the correct pages back each other up. This large sheet is then split, giving two copies of the completed section. With halfsheetwork (or 'work and turn') no economy can be effected through confining colour to one side of the paper.

Of the remaining means of binding sheets, the most important is section-sewn, which applies to full-scale books and is outside our present scope.

Flexiback (or perfect) binding consists of single leaves glued together at the back by special adhesive. It is much in evidence in paperbacks, being cheap if impermanent. Its chief value in general work is for pads—the top sheet can easily be removed without tearing. It can sometimes be used instead of a perforation.

Loose-leaf systems of binding are many, each with its own special requirements which must be met by the designer. All need considerable extra space at the binding edge, which makes normal margins impracticable. The alternatives to conventional margins are investigated in the next section. Loose-leaf bindings are often expensive and are employed when the removal and addition of single pages is an essential requirement of the job. When it is particularly desirable to have the pages of a job open very flat, or even to fold right back, as in a calendar, a form of loose-leaf is adopted, such as spiral wire. Work printed throughout on board also demands this kind of binding.

38 unconventional margins

The two traditional ways of establishing satisfactory proportions between type area and paper are based on the simple optical needs of leaflet and book work respectively. It is arguable that multi-page work which does not fulfil a similar role to the book need not adhere slavishly to its design principles. In certain circumstances, for example, with some forms of binding, notably loose-leaf, conventional margins are indeed not possible. Likewise, in stabbed work, pages have to be held firmly at the foredges to open them sufficiently for reading. The same is true of all booklets which have large pages, whatever the binding method. There is a good functional reason for making these foredge margins wider than the others.

Similar problems will be met with from time to time by the practising designer, but even when considerations of use and manufacture permit normal practice, it is possible to prefer on purely stylistic grounds proportions founded on the principles of asymmetric design.

Once a decision has been made to adopt unconventional page layout, for whatever cause, it is best to begin by drawing within the usual trimmed double spread a type area which observes ordinary single-page margins for each page. Make the margins rather narrower than customary. The extent of the area to be filled by the text can be decided by dividing this type area according to the requirements of the work and by the principles learned from sections 24 and 25. As the compositor will make up his pages to the full type area, the remaining space not occupied by text can be utilised in a number of ways typified under:

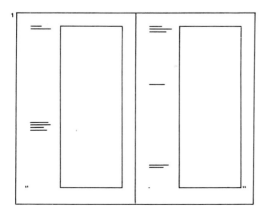
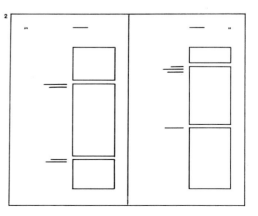

124

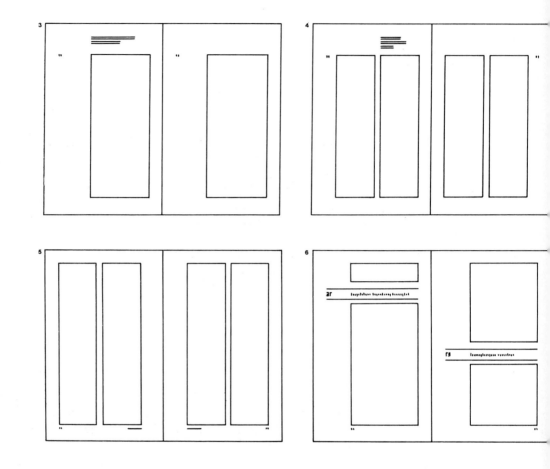

Figs. 1, 2, 3, 4 and 6 show some alternative treatments of section headings of varying importance. In fig. 4 the margins are eminently suited to stabbed work (note that in the diagram the space lost in the backs through stapling has not been made visible). The arrangement in fig. 5 is typical of loose-leaf work. A variety of suggestions for folio position are made throughout the figures. These page layouts are not to be accepted as ready-made answers; on the contrary, each job must be designed to solve its own unique set of problems.

Lund Humphries

Foreign language, scholarly and scientific publications

page 2 Arabic
4 Cantonese
6 Chinese
10 Modern Greek
10 Hebrew
11 Japanese
13 Polish
15 Portuguese
14 Russian
17 Spanish
18 Turkish
19 Structure drill through speech patterns
21 Scholarly publications
23 Witwatersrand University Press Publications
24 World Power Conference Publications

Fifty Chinese Stories

Selected from Classical Texts, romanized and translated into Modern Chinese
by Y. C. Liu
Lecturer in Chinese, School of Oriental and African Studies, University of London
With an introduction and romanized Japanese versions
by W. Simon, Dr.Phil., D.Lit., F.B.A.
Emeritus Professor of Chinese in the University of London

1960. Demy 8vo
256 pages
45s

In this book, Classical Chinese is approached through the medium of the modern spoken language. Each classical passage is accompanied by a modern version and a romanized Japanese version. Both Chinese versions are romanized according to the Gwoyeu-Romatzyh system, and through marking the beginning of the numbered lines of the Chinese text by superior figures attached to the respective romanized word in each of the three romanizations, an easy reference from the character text to the romanizations and vice versa has been made possible. In the Introduction the student will find detailed instructions as to how best to use the book and thereby lay a sound foundation for acquiring Classical Chinese. Great care has been taken to match the classical version by a modern rendering that is not only accurate but also fully acceptable from the point of view of style. As is implied in the title of the book the selected classical passages are all in narrative style and the modern versions may therefore be studied (and enjoyed) also by students of the modern language who may prefer to use this book simply as a collection of Chinese stories written in modern Chinese.
For the first ten lessons 'Vocabularies and Notes' have been added to give the student further guidance. English translations are available of thirty of the fifty stories, and students are referred to these translations in a 'Finding List' appended at the end of the book.

1948 (rev. ed. 1959)
Crown 8vo. 112 pages
6s See page 19

1956. Demy 8vo
200 pages
45s

Structure Drill in Chinese

W. Simon, Dr.Phil., D.Lit., F.B.A., and T. C. Chao, LL.B.

Two Chinese Philosophers

Ch'eng Ming-tao and Ch'eng Yi-ch'uan

A. C. Graham, B.A., Ph.D.
Lecturer at the School of Oriental and African Studies, University of London

There are two great periods in the history of Chinese thought, the latter part of the Chou dynasty (c.500-221 B.C.) and the Sung dynasty (A.D.960-1279). The Chinese thinkers best known in Europe are those of the first period and they are moralists, mystics, and political theorists rather than philosophers. This book is an account of the work of the brothers Ch'eng Ming-tao and Ch'eng Yi-ch'uan, who have good claims to be considered the most creative of the Neo-Confucian philosophers of the Sung dynasty.

Pages from a publisher's catalogue
by Lund Humphries

---

63 GARSCUBE ROAD 1944-45
Board, 30 x 38
Inscr. 'Macdonald' b.r, and 'Tom Macdonald/Garscube Road' on verso
Another view from the studio windows at Grovepark Street
Lent by the artist

64 TRANSPORT DEPOT 1944-45
Oil on paper, 20 x 22
Not inscribed
The old Townhead Goods Depot, near Buchanan Street Station
Lent by the artist

65 THE BIG GAME c1945
Pastel, 14½ x 19
Inscr. 'Macdonald' t.l.
A crowd at a football match
Lent by the artist

MARGARET Morris (born 1891) Ballet dancer and painter. Trained under Raymond Duncan, and founded the Margaret Morris Movement for naturalistic dancing. Encouraged to paint by J. D. Ferguson in Paris 1913 and later became his wife. Between 1925-39 founded five training schools in Britain and one in Paris. Moved to Glasgow 1939, started the Celtic Ballet in 1940.

66 ANITA AND MYSELF 1921
Canvas, 25 x 30
Inscr. with artist's name and address on verso
Exh: 4th NSG, May 1946 (46); NSG Retrospective, April 1955 (1) with date as 1916
Lent by the artist

67 ROSE AND VOSLIN 1922
Board, 23½ x 10½
Inscr. 'Margaret Morris 1922' on verso
Exh: 1st NSG, April 1943 (47) as 'Voslin'
Lent by the artist

68 THE QUARRY, 'WERNFAUR', HARLECH c1921
Board, 10½ x 13½
Inscr. 'Margaret Morris Quarry "Wernfaur" ' on verso
Exh: 2nd NSG, May 1944 (16) as 'The Quarry, "Wernfaur"'
Lent by the artist

JOHN Morrison (born 1904) Trained as an instrument maker, which is still his main occupation. Studied art at Working-men's Club in early 1930's, with two years' evening classes in the Life School at Glasgow School of Art c1938-40. Showed once at the RSA 1943, before becoming founder member of the NSG.

69 THE POLISHING SHOP 1943
Board, 11 x 15½
Inscr. with artist's name and title on verso
Repr: Ferguson, The New Scottish Group (1947), pl.31
A study for the larger painting of the same title shown at the 2nd NSG, May 1944 (20)
Lent by the artist

70 DESIGN 1944
Canvas laid on board, 18 x 21
Not inscribed
Coll. Purchased from the artist 1944
Exh: 2nd NSG, May 1944 (47)
Repr: Ferguson, The New Scottish Group (1947), colour pl.29
Lent by Glasgow Art Gallery and Museum (2374)

BETTY Simpson (1903-1960) Studied briefly at Heatherley's Art School 1921, then studied painting and design with Margaret Morris and Ferguson, in relation to dancing. Designed costumes and décor for her own dance compositions. Founder member of the New Art Club. Founded, with Anne Cornock-Taylor, Margaret Morris Movement school in London c1950.

71 STILL LIFE WITH TEAPOT c1940
Canvas, 20 x 24
Not inscribed
Lent by Miss Anne Cornock-Taylor

72 CONNEMARA LANDSCAPE c1940-45
Watercolour, 12½ x 15½
Not inscribed
Lent by Miss Anne Cornock-Taylor

NOTE A selection of documentary material, photographs, catalogues, minute books and press cuttings are displayed in show cases in this exhibition

Pages from an exhibition catalogue
for Scottish Arts Council

Make a specimen double spread layout for the text pages of a periodical for a professional institute. It is likely to run to a maximum of 48 text pages, saddle-stitched, and the page size asked for is A4. Running heads, folios and a specimen article heading are to be designed. The running head consists of the magazine's title with month and year of publication. The article heading comprises a title whose length will vary up to a maximum of ten words, the author's name and degrees, and a short introductory paragraph. Specify the paper.

It would be most realistic to begin this exercise by making up a dummy of the text pages of the magazine with the correct number of pages, style of binding and using the actual paper or one very similar to it. In choosing the paper assume that quality is important in this kind of work, that no illustrations are present, but that minimum weight consistent with opacity and good page handling characteristics is wanted to keep down postal charges. When, a here, the magazine is sent to members by post, it is common practice to weigh the dummy (plus cover and packaging) and check against the rates in *The Post Office Guide*.

In a page size as large as A4, the line length of the text when set in a reasonable size of type would much exceed the three or so alphabets which is usually recommended as the maximum measure for purposes of readability. While one of the main advantages of unconventional margins is that they reduce the measure of the text matter in a larger format to more acceptive limits, in this instance more words per page would be obtained by using two columns, but again placed unconventionally.

Relatively narrow measures have the advantage, from an editorial point of view, of giving the reader the illusion of reading faster and therefore more easily—as in newspapers. However, very short measures are tiring to read for any length of time and lead to too many word breaks and irregularities in word spacing. A space of an em, two at most, is enough to separate the columns visually. The space between columns must be less than any margin. No dividing rule is needed.

As regards page layout, it is best to experiment on a random selection of people with the dummy copy, to discover where they tend to hold the pages open, and whether additional marginal space is required for this. Column length in an A4 page is excessive and it is worth debating whether the text should be dropped from the head in the manner of figs. 3 and 4 above.

When designing the specimen article heading the main question to be settled is whether it is to occupy the width of one or both columns. The latter may be preferred when the articles are few and lengthy, as it gives the title more prominence, but emphasis can also be lent to a single-column heading

Client's layout (opposite)
and trial printed spread
for the magazine of
Institute of Chartered
Accountants of Scotland
*Alterations in detail were made
before the final printing*

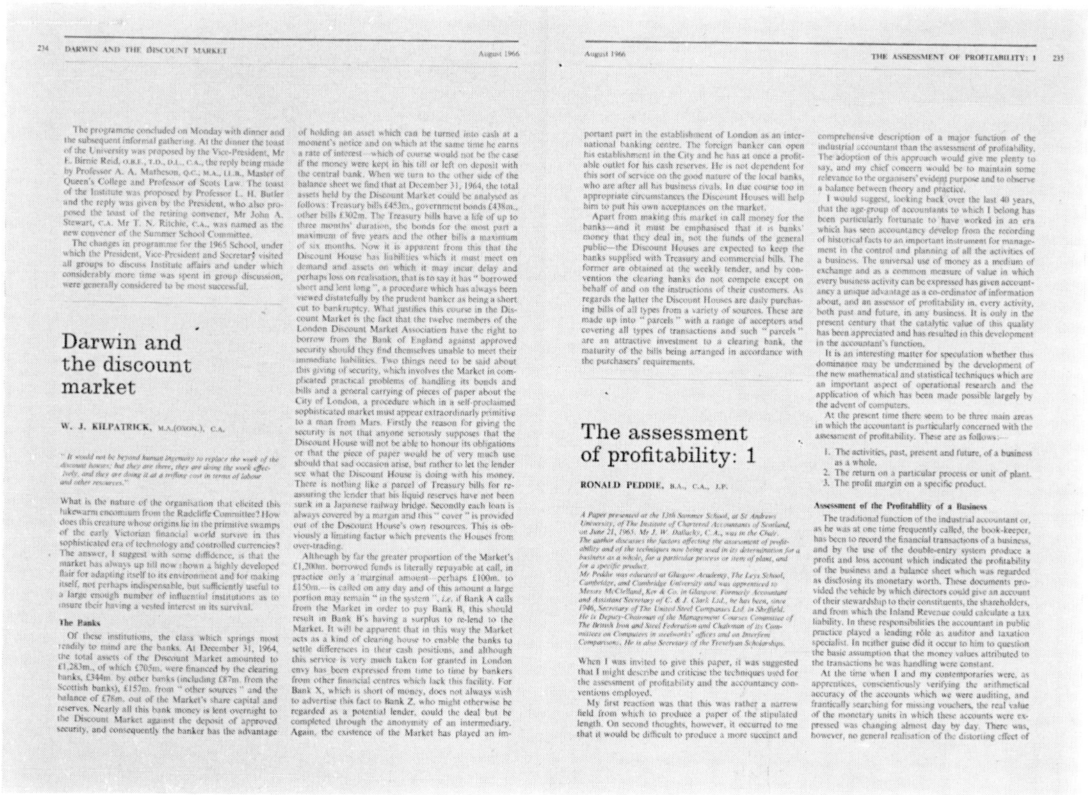

Darwin and
the discount
market

W. J. KILPATRICK, M.A.(OXON.), C.A.

The assessment
of profitability: 1

RONALD PEDDIE, B.A., C.A., J.P.

by using the means explored in earlier lessons—notably rules, white space and display faces. Single-column headings have the added attractions of editorial flexibility and simpler make-up.

Running heads are occasionally useful in periodicals and are mandatory if the periodical is registered with the Post Office as a newspaper. They should be unobtrusive and there seems to be no reason why they should not be put at the foot of the page. Folios must be easily found when thumbing through the pages, but must not complicate make-up. Compare the usefulness of the different folio positions indicated in the previous figures.

In your working layout, list full instructions for mechanical composition including details of the style to be adopted for the author's name and degrees and the introductory paragraph.

Cover printed black and mauve and page printed in red from a loose-leaf products list for Thomas Morson using perspex spring binder

39 applying a grid system

Present-day typographic style originated in twentieth-century painting and sculpture and in the parallel movements in architecture and industrial design. One of the ideas imported from modern architecture was mentioned in section 35: the limitation of choice through standardization, in order to produce in quantity with subsequent economic benefits.

The architect Le Corbusier in his book *The Modulor* proposed a series of mathematically related measurements based on the human figure, whose use he claimed would at the same time facilitate mass production and result in aesthetically pleasing proportions throughout a structure. This is the concept behind the module: a basic measure from which a restricted range of proportionally related measurements may be derived.

In print the methods of manufacture do not encourage as thorough or complex a use of the module as do architecture and some other design fields, though the advantages of standardizing certain elements of the page have been stressed. In multi-page work, for instance, standardization of page size and the major typographic measurements is advisable. Limitations on typeface, size and to a lesser extent measure were set by the mechanical composing machines. But the total application of a proportional system to the printed page remains more a stylistic preference than a necessity of economic production.

Proportion plays a vital part in asymmetric design, which, owing to the nature of type and the conventions of reading, as well as to contemporary taste, are superimposed on structures of intersecting vertical and horizontal straight lines. The success of a layout, in purely formal terms, depends greatly on the proportions created throughout it. A modular system carries this further by imposing strict relationships between all the main measurements on the page and seeking to establish them mathematically.

The basic measurement, usually the type measure, becomes the module from which the other divisions of the page area—page depth, margins, illustrations etc—and the paper size itself are derived by applying a ratio. Because of the change of scale, ratios based on the human figure cannot have the validity which they possess in architecture, and indeed the simplest proportions—1:2, 1:3 or 2:3—are often the most satisfactory in practice on the printed page. Examine the diagrams overleaf.

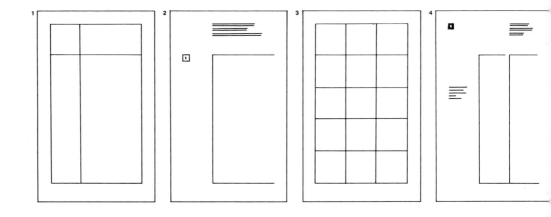

Fig. 1 is a simple structure as employed in previous asymmetric exercises
while fig. 2 shows the possible appearance of a printed page formed upon it.
A more elaborate grid calculated on modular principles and embodying
proportions of 1:1, 3:1 and 3:5 is illustrated in fig. 3, with its printed equiv
alent in fig. 4. Note that typographic elements are placed only where a vertical
meets a horizontal on the grid.

One grid of this sort permits a great variety of possible layouts. In multi
page work the imaginative use of a single grid serves to provide diversity of
effect from one spread to the next, while ensuring that all pages retain a basic
unity. When a large number of pages is involved, however, it may be ad
visable to employ two or even three basic grids.

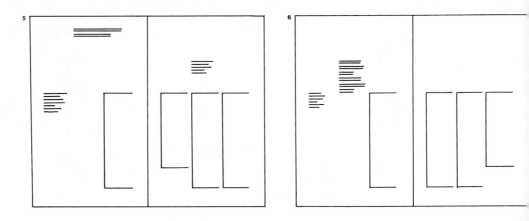

Figs. 5 and 6 are constructed on the same grid as fig. 4 and should prove that
far from being a restriction on the designer and ending in predictable same
ness, the system is a means of preserving an underlying order while permitting
greater freedom of imagination than ever. In addition to the usual two
principal axes, there is now the opportunity of using subsidiary axes. In the

above figures the principal vertical and horizontal axes are still seen to be the most important. But subsidiary horizontal and subsidiary vertical axes have also been made use of in the layout. The boundaries of the type area are themselves part of the grid and the spaces between columns must also be drawn into the grid. Thus more complex and subtle spatial relationships are made possible.

While the technique is of most value in the appearance and to a lesser degree the production of multi-page work, it can be extended to other print, as in the letterheading below, based on a grid of carefully proportioned rectangles:

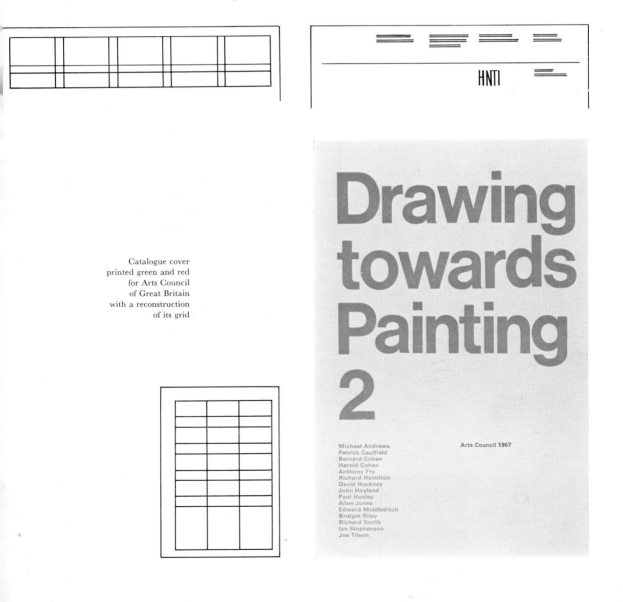

Catalogue cover
printed green and red
for Arts Council
of Great Britain
with a reconstruction
of its grid

All these spreads
from a Wiggins Teape
directors' report
are derived from
one grid

Wiggins Teape offer the most diverse choice of paper backed by the finest sales service.

And even a bit of paper has to be sold. Production comes before delivery but it does not come before sales; it is profitless to make what cannot be sold.

Recently Wiggins Teape gave their customers the most comprehensive set of paper samples the world has ever seen. There were 1,372 samples of paper and board in a unique collection. The range extended beyond what is made in the Group's own mills, because the Group's merchanting organisation sells half as much again. In the United Kingdom there are 12 sales branches and there are 32 spread across the world. The home branches sell on the average 1,500 items a week and they have in stock 2,000 different items. This diversity of paper

Prompt delivery is assured by a fleet of vehicles operating from the many branches of the Wiggins Teape Group.

carried in stock is vital, for a customer likes to feel he has a complete choice. The branches' task is to provide the right paper at the right time at the right price.

Each UK branch is self-contained and of a size to match the printing industry it serves. The larger branches are in London, Bristol, Birmingham, Leeds, Manchester, Nottingham and Liverpool—cities where printing is a major industry. Sales representatives call on printers large and small. In a confined commercial centre like Cardiff, a representative might call on ten prospective customers in a day . In the more isolated parts of Wales a man might call on only three. Among them the branches cover the country from Land's End beyond John of Groats to the Shetland Islands. In a programme of modernisation and enlargement, branches at Liverpool, Bristol and London are next in line for development.

An important proportion of sales are made over the telephone. Trained salesmen man the telephone at every branch, and customers have come to value a quick answer on availability and price and a promise of delivery that can be relied on. Some of the telephone salesmen are as well known to buyers by their voices as are their counterparts who sell face to face.

The branches recruit their staffs locally and they have an advantage which is implicit in the breadth of the Group. A promising new recruit attends training school at head office, spends time at a paper mill and later he is liable to be promoted anywhere in the world of Wiggins Teape.

Speciality papers are sold by speciality salesmen. These men invade the most unlikely places. Recently a Wiggins Teape salesman visited a steel mill with the hope, but little expectation, of finding an industrial use for paper there. He found one.

Wiggins Teape exports, which were at a record level in 1964, have been rising ever since the Boer war and today the Group exports one fifth of what it makes—to 122 countries. Exports are not just fun. They are work and enterprise and patience. Like the grass of an Oxford quadrangle they have to be tended over the years to achieve their full maturity. The 30 fully-fledged, stock-carrying branches overseas have grown from 10 before the 1939 war. If the range of paper dealt in at a U.K. branch is diverse, the range of an overseas branch is more so. The overseas representatives sell superb "Goatskin" parchment paper at a top price, down to the

cheapest newsprint—and they handle the sales of a lot of paper made by mills outside the Group. They also deal in non-paper lines such as printing machines. Their supplies of paper come from the U.K. and—increasingly—from Wiggins Teape mills in the countries the branches are selling in : economic nationalism is the trend of the time and indigenous products have no tariff barriers to leap.

In Australia, for instance, the output of four paper machines at Wiggins Teape's mill on the Shoalhaven river is sold through the Company's branches at Sydney, Melbourne, Adelaide, Perth and Brisbane, as well as through other Australian paper merchants. And the Indian mill makes cigarette paper for India, as well as for export markets ranging from Fiji to Zanzibar.

The exports of Wiggins Teape and their earnings of foreign currency go some way to reduce the imbalance of the Group's exports and imports. Added to the contribution of home-made pulp from the Sudbrook mill they reduce Wiggins Teape's trade gap to a degree remarkable in the British paper industry.

Paper mills are at the centre of Wiggins Teape's world - fifteen of them in the United Kingdom and there are mills in four continents. The range of papers produced is enormous. Wiggins Teape make a wider range of paper than any other paper-maker in the world and the speed of the machines making it is increasing all the time. Everywhere science is finding its way into the mills, helping to make better paper faster.

The Mills themselves are very diverse in size, equipment and output. They range from the largest, Dartford and Greaseproof Mills, which includes the large Number 6 machine 180 inches wide, running at over 1,000 feet per minute, to Ivybridge Mill in Devon, whose two small machines produce the special paper required for postage stamps and Postal Orders.

Top left Bridgend Paper Mills—jointly owned with Smith & Nephew Associated Companies Limited

Top right Mechanical handling of material and paper aids efficiency

Above Reels of tissue in store

Bottom Left Jonathan—The mighty Yankee machine at Bridgend

30

31

The other mills are scattered across the country. Their only common factor is proximity to a plentiful supply of clean water, for when the pulp goes on the machine it forms one per cent of a mixture that is 99 per cent water. These mills are at Chartham, Chorley, Bury in Lancashire, where there are two, Hele in Devon, Dover, High Wycombe in Buckinghamshire, Sunderland and St. Mary Cray in Kent. Speedy delivery of paper in suitable quantities from these mills to home buyers is a service which papermakers in the forest lands cannot match.

Left Glory Mill, High Wycombe

Top centre Water is basic to papermaking

Centre Hylton Mill, Sunderland

Bottom centre Devon Valley Mill, Exeter, Devon

Right Washing paper after parchmentising

Bottom right Chartham Mill, near Canterbury, Kent

34

35

Using a grid, design a title page and specimen illustrated double spread for a book, maximum untrimmed size Crown 4to, oblong format, printed black only on coated paper. Sanserif set in several columns is asked for and allowance should be made for folios and frequent sub-headings. Copy for the title-page is : 'J. Müller-Brockmann/*The graphic artist and his design problem*/Creative problems of the graphic designer/Design and training in commercial art/Alec Tiranti/London'.

The practice recommended to the student of beginning with the design of the main text areas now becomes absolutely essential. Start by drawing out the double spread to maximum trimmed dimensions and thinking of a possible typeface, point size, leading, number and measure of columns, with margins. Draw the probable positions of the columns very lightly on the double spread.

At this point no precise proportions have yet been established, decisions having been made on considerations of legibility and practicality. Now this suggested paper size and layout is to be modified so that certain mathematical relationships are formed between the module (single-column type measure) and all other major measurements. This can be done by dividing up the type area of the page into rectangles based on the module, as discussed earlier. Column depth, illustrations and position of display elements will conform to this grid.

A grid is not determined in isolation from the problems presented by the copy and the nature of the job, and the type then forced to fit it. On the contrary, an individual grid scheme must be worked out for each job, after due attention has been paid to its particular requirements. That is why this

Cover and spread
for a booklet
designed on a grid

exercise began, not with the grid itself, but with the normal procedure whose provisional findings can now be modified to create a modular grid.

The simplest and in many ways the most useful manner of dividing a type area is to break it up into squares, as was done in figs. 3 to 6. A series of simple relationships can then be built up between type measure, page width and depth, and paper proportions. A more complex division of the page, as adopted in several of the illustrations, involving various sizes of rectangles and less simple ratios, can be made if desired and if the copy warrants it. For a fuller discussion of mathematical series as used in the division of areas consult Sausmarez: *Basic design*, chapter 3, and Ghyka: *Geometrical composition and design*.

Some typographers find definite mathematical relationships for even the smallest measurements in the grid: for example, margins and the space between columns, but this is not easy if em sizes are to be kept to. In any case it is doubtful if such small measurements are perceptible as proportions of the module at all. In the present exercise it is enough to relate measure, column depth, page width and depth, and if possible paper size. Draw a suitable grid on the double spread layout and erase all traces of the provisional one.

When treatment of folios and sub-headings has been marked-up, indicate by shaded areas possible placings and sizes of three photographic illustrations of varying proportions. Their dimensions must conform to the grid but any of them may be wider than a single column. Simple fractions of the module are occasionally used to introduce variety and to preserve the shape of an original photograph.

Study the illustrations before continuing. In this similar design problem all pages adhere to the selfsame grid established for the text pages. Examples of contemporary applications of the system as illustrated in current graphic design periodicals should also be sought at this stage. Then proceed with the preparation of a working layout for the title page, again over the grid which has been made for the text pages. The layout may be extended over a double spread if desired.

135

Prepare a working layout for a letter-heading, size A4, printed in two workings, for a periodical called *Graphics*. The rest of the copy is: 'International journal for the graphic arts/Graphic Press/54 Russell Square, London W1C 3RA/Telephone 041–405 2367/Telegrams Graphics, London/ Editor: Charles Nash, BA, FSIA'. Base your layout on a grid scheme. Give full details of paper and inks.

A leaflet is distinct from a booklet in that it consists of one sheet of paper only and therefore does not require binding. By folding several times a leaflet can be made to do the same job as a small booklet without the cost of securing sheets together. In addition, a number of interesting effects can be obtained. Some common folds are:

Fig. 1 represents a common 4pp folder, fig. 2 the popular 6pp format. The zigzag or concertina fold in fig. 3 can be extended to comprise many more pages, one of 8pp being shown as fig. 4. Other variations can be worked out on this basis, with the provision that the number and direction of folds is dependent on the capabilities of the folding machine to be used. The direction of the grain of the paper and its substance are other technical factors which the printer must consider. Creasing on a letterpress printing machine before folding is necessary with heavy papers and all boards.

Besides number and direction of folds, size and shape have a bearing on the handiness of a folder. Size depends on standard sheet size available and on the functional requirements of the work. Folders often have to fit the pocket or an envelope, and when fully opened the sheet must not be unwieldy.

The cinematographic effect of the sequence of pages in multi-page jobs has been remarked upon. In folders of more than four pages a certain added subtlety occurs. Consider fig. 2 above. As always the cover serves to attract attention and to stimulate interest. The reader next sees, not the inside spread, but pages 2 and 5 together. Then he turns the flap and reads pages 2, 3 and 4. Page 6 is rather difficult to find and should for this reason be left blank or allotted quite unimportant copy.

The information put on page 5 must be such as justifies its presentation in front of the main matter on the final three-page spread, but which will not then be badly missed on its disappearance when the flap is turned. The wording on page 2 must make sense when read along with that on page 5, and again when in conjunction with pages 3 and 4. It will be appreciated that close attention to the sense of the copy and its intelligent allocation over the available pages are the most vital essentials to the success of a folder as a method of communication.

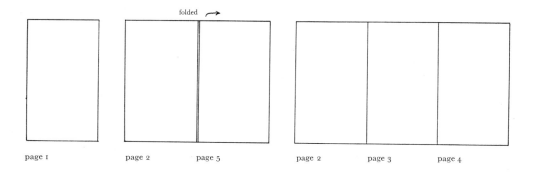

folded →

page 1   page 2   page 5   page 2   page 3   page 4

Keeping in mind that unity is ensured only by treating as a whole all that is visible at one time, the approach to a folder as illustrated above must be to design pages 2 and 5 as a loosely linked double spread, and pages 2, 3 and 4 as another spread. Now apply these general principles in an exercise.

138

**the
view**

**the
view
you are
about
to see
may
save
your life...**

**the
view
you are
about
to see
may
save
your life...**

**keep it
clear
with a
Triplex
self-heated
rear window**

permanent built in

defrosting + demisting

In mist, frost, ice, freezing rain and snow, only a
Triplex electrically heated rear window keeps
crystal clear inside and out. The Triplex heated
window proved in Rolls-Royce and Bentley is now
available for most current cars. A clear rear view
at all times is vital to your safety. Think of the
benefits! Relaxed control. No wondering who is
'on your tail' or whether it is safe to make a turn.

by Triplex!

Specification: Voltage 12v. Rating 30 watts per
sq. ft. Consumption 5 amps approx. Element: almost invisible Tungsten wire embedded in glass.

Advertising folder
printed red and black
for Triplex:
zigzag fold

Folder printed in red
for the Society
of Typographic Designers:
zigzag fold

std programme 67/68

repare working layouts for a 6pp
older printed in black and one colour,
f a size suitable for pocketing and
osting. List paper, envelope and ink.
he copy is: 'National Orchestra Club/
eason 19xx–x/Supported by the
rts Council of Great Britain/Concert
rogramme/All meetings at 7.30 pm
n the Concert Hall, Smith Street/
onorary chairman: Sir James Pelman
BE/Honorary secretary: Charles
winburne, JP/Programme/

uesday 27 September
Serenade concert by the National
Chamber Orchestra/Conductor
James Gibb

uesday 8 November
The language of music: lecture/
Speaker: Sir Maurice Bell

uesday 22 November
Recital of works by Haydn,
Beethoven, Liszt and Bartok/Piano:
Marie Parkhouse

Monday 12 December
Recital of works by Mozart,
Beethoven and Brahms/David Cross,
violin/Hugh Alexander, piano

hursday 2 February
Lieder recital/Robert Duncan, tenor/
Alan Davis, piano

uesday 7 March
Choral concert by the Consort
Singers/Conductor: John Weight

hursday 6 April
Chamber concert by the Allwyn
Trio/Works by Boccherini, Mozart
and Schubert/Peter Crawford,
violin/Charles Chalmers, viola/Jack
Jones, violoncello

pplication for membership to the
reasurer and Secretary, Miss R.J.
acobson, 75 Mill Drive/Annual
ubscription 75p/Life membership
5. 50p/Junior membership, open to
tudents and schoolchildren, 15p/
Member's levy at each meeting 10p/
uests 25p/Additional facilities avail-
ble to club members such as priority
ooking and visits to musical events,
ttendance at rehearsals and special
usical evenings'.

Use a grid system if wanted. In either case begin by allotting the copy to specific pages, using the minimum on the cover and leaving the last page blank. Then work out an appropriate and economic format.

The first pages to be tackled will be those devoted to the details of the actual programme and, as these are tabular in form and their presentation above not to be taken as a guide, reference once more to section 33 will be helpful. Design the cover last, because it offers few problems and asks for an imaginative approach. As the function of the outside of the folder in this instance is not mainly informative, but is intended to stimulate interest and remain memorable for recognition purposes throughout the season, a freer solution than usual may be sought.

Both sides of a zig-zag folder
printed in olive
for Association of Teachers
of Printing and Allied Subjects

140

Scottish Opera Spring 1968

Perth Theatre	April 9	The Marriage of Figaro
	10	Full Circle / The Soldier's Tale
	11	The Marriage of Figaro
	12	Full Circle / The Soldier's Tale
	13	Full Circle / The Soldier's Tale
Glasgow King's	May 3	Boris Godunov
	4	The Marriage of Figaro
	10	Boris Godunov
	11	Madama Butterfly
	14	Madama Butterfly
	15	Götterdämmerung
	16	The Marriage of Figaro
	mat. 17	The Marriage of Figaro
	17	Madama Butterfly
	18	Götterdämmerung
Aberdeen His Majesty's	May 21	Götterdämmerung
	22	The Marriage of Figaro
	23	Madama Butterfly
	24	The Marriage of Figaro
	25	Boris Godunov
Edinburgh King's	May 28	Boris Godunov
	29	Madama Butterfly
	30	The Marriage of Figaro
	mat. 31	The Marriage of Figaro
	31	Madama Butterfly
	June 1	Boris Godunov
	4	Götterdämmerung
	5	Boris Godunov
	6	The Marriage of Figaro
	7	Götterdämmerung
	8	The Marriage of Figaro

Further information from
Scottish Opera Limited
142 Holland Street, Glasgow C2
phone CENtral 5288

Small gummed sticker
printed in black
for Scottish Opera

In the past the typographer was concerned solely with typographic materials type, rule and border. Today he is expected also to have some skill in graphic work such as lettering and the devising and drawing of symbols. Since the reproduction of these involves photographic processes, some knowledge of techniques is desirable. Clowes: *A guide to printing*, chapter 4, covers the elements and Cannon, Wallis: *Graphic reproduction* provides information in depth.

The simplest use of process materials for letterpress printing is the solid. This is a flat piece of zinc, plastic or rubber cut to the required size and made up to type height so as to print an unbroken area of ink. If the shape is simple and rectangular, no artwork or camera need be involved, the plate being cut mechanically and cheaply. If the job is being printed by lithography, of which more will be said in sections 49 and 50, the method of printing is different but the preparation is identical. Sizes should be stated in millimetres.

Difficulties can be experienced when printing solids, especially large areas by letterpress on uncoated stock. If the paper surface is too uneven to allow bottoming of the grain, the result is mottled and unpleasant. No such difficulty occurs with lithography, which can print large solids successfully on most surfaces. In either process and on any stock, the amount of ink needed to give adequate coverage of large solid areas is likely to be too much for accompanying type. Small fine type nearby becomes in extreme cases quite illegible.

Another common fault is uneven inking of solids, when their extent is greater than one circumference of the rollers, due to the rollers having lost most of their ink before travelling over the furthest solid parts. Designs making excessive use of solids, particularly in small jobbing, may have to be revised in the light of this. It will also be found that more opaque inks are easier to print evenly than transparent inks.

Reverse line plates are solids with an image appearing as a non-printing area. It is useful on occasion to reinforce the impact of a type line by treating it in this way. A perfect machine-proof of the type on coated paper is necessary for the camera, with the extent of the plate marked. Same size is acceptable.

As with solids, there are limitations of stock and process on the use of reverse plates, with the added danger that fine recessed lines tend to fill with ink during the run, more so with uncoated stock. Even with coateds, very small or delicately formed typefaces, such as moderns, are difficult to print cleanly and legibly in reverse.

While plates with reversed type are employed usefully in work printed in black only, as an effective means of strengthening a heading or main line solids require to be printed in colour. Type overprinted in black or a colour on a solid area is subject to the laws of legibility stated in section 17. Reverse plates in colour must also be carefully examined from this point of view. A white image on a black background is as visible as black on white, more dramatic, but tiring to the eye if reading is prolonged. Reduction of tonal contrast between image and background by printing in colour or on a coloured paper needs bigger and bolder type as compensation.

Type in reverse and solids offer new ways of creating lively and interesting effects through variety of treatment within a layout. *A print user's guide to colour* shows type in reverse and overprinted in a wide range of colours, providing a valuable check on strength and legibility of lines so treated. Analysis of all the colour possibilities open when a single colour is available along with black reveals six combinations of image and background:

Institute of Printing bulletin
printed black and grey

type in black/white paper

type in colour/white paper

type reversed in black/white paper

type in black/solid in colour

type in colour/solid in black

type reversed in colour/white paper

    When type is to appear in colour against a black background, a simple overprint is impossible in the major printing processes, for reasons gone into in section 17 concerning translucency of inks. The effect is achieved by printing from two plates, first a solid in colour, then a reverse plate slightly larger (to avoid register problems) on top of it in black. The black obliterates the underlying colour except where the reversed type allows colour to show through. A side effect is that the double layer of ink takes on a gloss.

    Not all of the six combinations are feasible unless a middle value colour is chosen. A light or dark colour does not give the necessary tonal contrast in every case. Designs gain in visual interest as more of these contrasting effects are incorporated into them, just as alternation of alphabets produces variety

std

Society of Typographic Designers

Programme of meetings 1962-63

PROGRAMME OF MEETINGS FOR 1962–1963

std

The Society of Typographic Designers is a professional body of creative typographers and designers engaged in the Graphic Arts

Thursday 27 September at 6.30 pm	RISK EVERYTHING Frank Overton FSIA MSTD at Monotype House, Fetter Lane, London EC4
Thursday 25 October at 6.30 pm	TYPE DESIGN AND THE ROMAN LETTER Will Carter at Monotype House, Fetter Lane, London EC4
Thursday 29 November at 6.30 pm	HIM SPEAKS George Him FSIA at Overseas House, Park Place, London SW1
Thursday 31 January at 6.30 pm	ENGLISH SPEAKING TYPOGRAPHY Beatrice Warde at Overseas House, Park Place, London SW1
Thursday 28 February at 6.30 pm	DESIGN IN ENTERTAINMENT POSTERS George Mayhew at Monotype House, Fetter Lane, London EC4
Thursday 28 March at 6.30 pm	BEYOND THE CRINGE Michael Margolis MSTD MSIA at Overseas House, Park Place, London SW1
Thursday 25 April at 6.30 pm	TELEVISION GRAPHIC DESIGN Geoffrey Martin MSIA at Monotype House, Fetter Lane, London EC4
Thursday 16 May at 6.30 pm	THE TRAINING OF TYPOGRAPHERS Ian Bradbery FSIA at Monotype House, Fetter Lane, London EC4
Thursday 30 May at 6.30 pm	ANNUAL GENERAL MEETING AND ANNUAL DINNER (For members, wives and friends)

Principles

To endeavour to maintain the highest standards of design in the Graphic Arts. To further the development of graphic design by every possible means. To stimulate an appreciation of the importance of planned printing as an economic necessity of modern production. To encourage and advise those who wish to undertake a recognised course of study terminating in a certificated examination. To bring together creative typographers and designers to their mutual benefit and for the interchange of views, experiences, and to afford an opportunity for discussion of current work. To provide an up-to-date register of the special qualifications of members for the purpose of bringing them into contact with those who may require their services.

Particulars of membership may be obtained from the Hon. Secretary, R.W. Moulder, 67 Greenwood Road, Mitcham, Surrey.

Folder for the Society
of Typographic Designers
printed maroon and turquoise

In asymmetric design solid and reverse line plates are invaluable in giving maximum contrast of tone with unprinted areas and can be bled effectively in a manner similar to that proposed for rules in section 27. As rectangular units within the page, they are subject to the normal laws of proportion, not only with regard to their relationship with page proportions and axes, but also in the proportions of the plates themselves and the positions of type reversed on them.

When two or more translucent coloured inks are at the disposal of the designer, an additional colour may be obtained by overprinting. Endless opportunities for imaginative design are introduced by combining the possibilities of type, solids and reverse plates, in black, colour and overprinted.

The sketching of small-scale roughs and the visualisation of the printed result now become more difficult, however. Crayons, poster colours, and a range of felt-tipped pens are useful in different contexts, coloured gummed paper cuts quickly to give an accurate impression of solids, and where overprinting is contemplated coloured tissue, transfer colour and film such as Letraset Instant Colour and Letrafilm enable the designer to experiment in the initial stages. The medium selected for sketching roughs also suggests ways in which plates and colours can be combined. A change of medium often reveals new avenues of approach and the typographer should try to become equally proficient with all media for this reason. Some training in basic design is advisable before attempting complicated designs with these techniques. This is discussed in section 45.

Do not assume that any happy effect resulting from these media is automatically capable of being repeated by the printing process. In particular when overprinting translucent inks, the appearance of any rough must differ greatly from the printed end-product. Re-read section 21 and remember that only experience and intelligent examination of printed specimens can lead to success in this respect. See also Cooke: *Colour by overprinting*.

143

Using some or all of the media mentioned above, prepare a series of miniature sketches in colour for a booklet cover, trimmed size 200 × 140mm (8 × 5½in), to be printed on white ivory board. The copy is: 'BBC Radio for schools/Spring term/First half/9 January to 3 February'. Two workings additional to black are possible and use is to be made of solid and/or reverse plates to obtain as brightly attractive a cover as possible. Complete a caseroom layout in pencil of the most successful rough and list all specifications of letterpress inks and stock.

42 advertising

The impact of advertising on the appearance of print has been enormous. A
the start of last century the emergence of competitive print led first to th
invention of novel typeforms and then to experiments with the disposition o
the type on the page. Thus all print today, whatever its nature, is at leas
indirectly influenced by the techniques called into being by the needs o
advertising. Indeed, as the typography of the book dominated typographi
style in earlier centuries, so the visual effects proper to advertising are nov
carried into nearly every class of work.

The main difference between print which is essentially useful, informativ
or entertaining, and advertising—which may of course be all of these beside
—is the element of persuasion. Advertising seeks to stimulate the reader to
desired action—to buy a product or use a service—so that communicatio
becomes not merely a matter of informing, but of convincing.

The designer's contribution to this can be made only as one specialis
within a group. To play his part properly he must have a clear picture of th
whole situation.

First, he must know what the client hopes to achieve by the considerabl
expense often incurred. When no contact can be made with the advertise
himself, a close analysis of the copy supplied will reveal much, but only
proper briefing from the client or his representative can establish the condi
tions for a really effective design. The aims of advertising are varied: on
firm may want the immediate clearing of a load of cut-price goods; anothe
the long-term establishment of the firm's good name; yet another the creatio
of a favourable brand image, and so on. This aim must be defined, as it has
radical bearing on the presentation.

The means to be employed must be known. The advertiser will hav
chosen a particular method of approach—press advertisements, direct ma
shots, posters—whichever seems to him best suited to the purpose and th
market it is intended to reach. The designer has to be aware of the thinkin
which has led to the commissioning of the job in hand, and should b
acquainted with the client's other publicity, more so if it is only part of
larger campaign, so that he may win increased effectiveness from continuity o
style. A study of competitors' advertising is also useful background.

The typographer manipulates the visual aspects of words to make the
more comprehensible and to give them required impact. In advertising, whe
there is resistance on the part of the public to reading the copy at all, attrac
ing attention and arousing interest assume importance as well. In achievin
these ends the visual means at the disposal of the designer are restricted by th

levels of taste and visual awareness of the designated readership, which will rarely if ever coincide with those of the designer. In practice it is normally possible to keep up a respectable aesthetic standard while satisfying the needs of the job and its public.

Persuasion entails the communication of ideas with emotional associations or colouring. The feelings conveyed to the reader by copy, illustration and layout must be such that he is motivated in the way wanted by the advertiser. Investigations suggest that wording, over which the typographer has little or no control, is the most significant factor in the success of an advertisement. Illustration is next in importance and is mentioned in sections 45 to 48, while layout is the least effective persuader of the three. Nevertheless, the function of the layout in integrating the various parts of an advertisement into a meaningful whole, and in making the copy legible and intelligible is vital. It is worth remembering that it is the total impression of a piece of advertising which the reader absorbs.

In the following sections two aspects of advertising print are explored. There are many more, but the method of approach is the same for all and in conjunction with the information and practice gained elsewhere in the book, these sections should enable the student to tackle a wide range of advertising work. Wills: *The fundamentals of layout* is a useful guide to advertising techniques in typography.

Outside and opening spread
of a full-colour brochure
for Bergen Line

Newspaper advertising is one way of reaching a mass audience. Its main di
advantages from the designer's viewpoint are the limitations on quality ar
space imposed by technical and economic factors. Colour can hardly ever l
used and the coarseness of newsprint rules out fine illustration, except whe
the newspaper is produced by web offset.

The short life of a newspaper and the casual manner in which it tends
be read, together with the intense competition which an advertisement mu
contend with from surrounding editorial matter and other advertising on tl
large sheet, are additional problems for the designer. In these extreme
adverse conditions the message has to be seen, read and understood almo
instantaneously and without effort.

There are various ways of attracting attention to a press advertisement,
which sheer size is an obvious but expensive one. Unusual format ar
advantageous position on the page are matters for the space-buyer. Tl
inclusion of an arresting illustration is not one of the means discussed
present, being left until later. The resources remaining to the typographer a
two: namely, contrast and novelty.

The liveliness of appearance produced by contrast between typograph
elements can be pushed to its limits in advertising—though it must never l
permitted to reduce the legibility of the copy or disrupt the overall unity
style. Use of the more exotic display types and mixing together of unrelate
faces are practices which have their value in the ephemeral newspaper. N
where is the loss of the inflections of speech, inherent in its translation in
print, more serious than when the aim is persuasion. Typography must ofte
try to restore vocal expression by constant and appropriate variations of trea
ment in displayed matter, on the lines suggested below:

FLY BOAC TO USA

CARGO by sea

times change

Novelty and the curiosity aroused by the unexpected are potent devices which the designer can make use of. Although the generalizations made here about press advertising layout are essential for the student who wishes to learn its rudiments, it remains true that the advertisement which is in some way strikingly different—though in an acceptable way—is more likely to succeed in capturing an audience. Beware, however, of mere gimmickry which, unless it possesses the rare qualities of instant comprehensibility and genuine wit, will just as likely cheapen it, impede communication and alienate 147 the reader.

A decided contrast in tonal value between the area of the advertisement and surrounding text causes the eye to single it out. Either a very light overall impression, as in fig. 1 under, or a comparatively dark appearance, as in fig. 2, has this result, but in both instances snags arise. The existence of a high proportion of white space is only feasible when copy is brief and suitable, while a very black treatment can destroy legibility and for technical reasons publications are not keen to accept the more extreme examples.

Some of the advantages of both can be gained by allowing space all round the type matter, isolating the advertisement from its environment. At the same time a similar allocation of space around the main heading serves to make it stand out in relief. The effect is enhanced and the benefits of concentration of black enjoyed if a bold letter is specified. Provided it is limited to the heading, a reverse line plate offers density without loss of legibility.

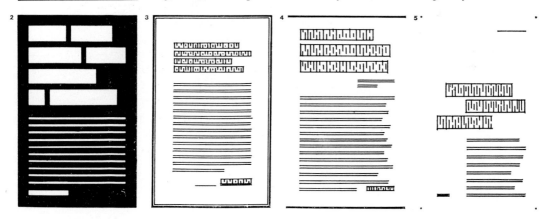

Rules separate and emphasize, whether printed all round the advertisement as in figs. 1 and 3 or, when space is scarce, confined to top and bottom as in fig. 4. The same purpose is served by strong, geometric ornament. Rules when used, should be placed at the extreme edges of the area paid for, but in no circumstances should type ever touch any of these edges, being always set back a little to provide a marginal space which would not otherwise exist. When, as in fig. 5, considerable space is left between the maximum area and the actual type, it is a useful practice to insert small dots at the corners to mark the limits.

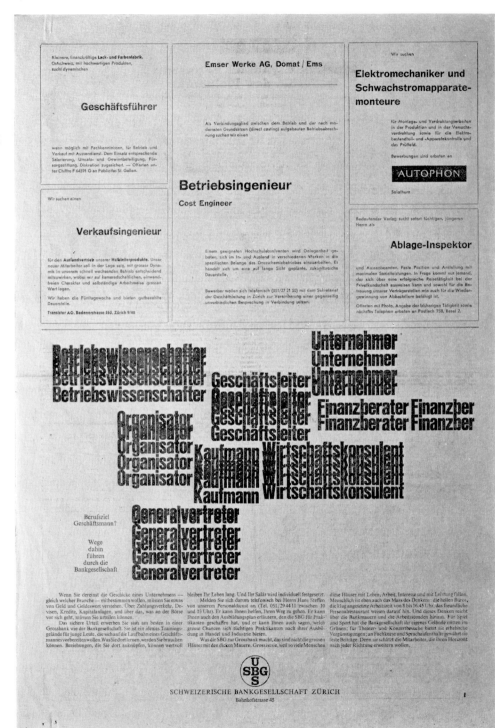

Examination of the make-up of newspapers reveals that fine separation rules are likely to be inserted as a matter of course close to the sides, top and bottom of each advertisement. Inclusion of rules in the interior of the advertisement is therefore better avoided, because the unity of the whole tends to be destroyed.

With attention attracted to the advertisement and interest aroused by a certain liveliness in the heading, it is imperative that no obstacle to the quick assimilation of the message is put in the way of the reader. His interest may be limited and he can easily be discouraged from reading by the slightest difficulty. The layout must at first glance give the impression of being simple, orderly and unified, with particular attention paid to logical grouping and relative emphasis.

Continuous text should be set in a readable face of an apparent size similar to that used editorially. Inessential copy must be ruthlessly reduced in size if it is not to confuse the basic message. Where the copywriter has recognized that many people scan an advertisement without reading the text, and has written his main lines so that they are intelligible when read on their own, the typographer should design with this in mind.

Subtleties of typeform, spacing and proportion are unlikely to help communication in the context of the newspaper page. Here it is more important to make clear the normal reading path from top to bottom, and not to introduce unnatural transitions between groups, however clever and superficially attractive the layout may seem, Examine, nevertheless, the page from the Swiss quality weekly *Die Weltwoche* illustrated. It demonstrates that high design standards can improve, rather than hinder, impact and legibility in favourable circumstances.

Advertising space in a newspaper is sold by the column width, depth being quoted in inches. Column measures vary between publications and are not necessarily in even ems. Relevant production information is to be had from the advertising department of the newspaper concerned. A printed copy does not provide absolutely accurate measurements, owing to the shrinkage which takes place during stereotyping prior to printing, about 1pt per inch.

Advertisements for insertion can either be house-set by the newspaper, or trade-set by a printer or specialist trade typesetter. The first method is quicker and probably cheaper and may have to be utilised when time is short, but newspapers do not carry a range of types beyond those customarily used for editorial copy and small ads, so selection has to be made from their specimen books. Setting is by line composition. Again, pressure of production does not allow that attention to typographic detail and careful interpretation of layout which is the mark of a good printer or typesetting service.

Layouts set by a typesetting service are likely to be more expensive but are free from the other limitations. When an advertisement is to be run in several different publications simultaneously, this method of setting is always chosen, duplicate plates being made of the type after it has been passed as satisfactory, and sent to the publications involved. If stereotypes are ordered the original layout and setting should be made proportionately larger than the actual size wanted, to allow for the shrinkage mentioned earlier. No shrinkage takes place in the case of electrotype plates. Information on duplicate plates is given in chapter 4 of Clowes: *A guide to printing* and elsewhere.

A growing number of newspapers are now produced by web-offset lithography. This process often allows the designer greater freedom and more direct control over the appearance of an advertisement, which can be sent to the newspaper as finished artwork, preferably same size, with pasted-up type pulls, ready for make-up into the newspaper page prior to photographing and platemaking. Any number of duplicates can be made photographically. See also section 49.

The student is also advised to read Day: *The typography of press advertisement* which investigates the subject in depth. In a field so influenced by passing fashions, however, *current* specimens of press advertising must ever be the main study.

Prepare a working layout for a single-column 5in advertisement for insertion in a local evening newspaper with a column measure of 11 ems 9pts. The setting is to be carried out by trade typesetter and the copy is: 'Sunday wines at Saturday prices/The man who enjoys good wine and takes an intelligent interest in what he drinks chooses from the stocks in our bins/ *400 characters of text follow*/The Vineyard Vaults/Call personally and sample our stock at 39 Samuel Street or telephone your order to 646 1245'.

The outstanding problem in the design of this advertisement is how to reconcile the need for high impact imposed by the medium, with the sophistication appropriate to the potential market. If you can have the layout set, proof it on newsprint, glue it in position on a page from an actual evening paper and try to assess how successful it is likely to be. Does it attract attention? Will it persuade?

Prepare a layout for setting by the newspaper for a double-column ($24\frac{1}{2}$ ems) 7in advertisement in the same publication as above. Copy consists of: 'Levis Brothers/Sale/ Sensational reductions in all departments/Opening Monday 3rd January at 9 a.m./*24 bargain items are listed, each similiar to this specimen*: 3-piece suites/Walnut, sapele, teak, oak, in traditional and contemporary designs. Formerly £95 to £110, to clear at £75/ 105 Main Street'.

Comparison with the preceding exercise shows that while the medium is unchanged, the market addressed is strikingly different. In this kind of advertising the word 'Sale' is a powerful eye-stopper and must be given as much prominence as possible. Throughout, boldness and size are more suitable than space as a means of emphasis, although the unrelenting blackness usually seen in this type of work surely defeats itself. The items for sale should be set in an orderly manner, legibly and without fuss, with the sale price displayed as large as convenient. The general effect aimed at is 'sensational' and the typographer's job is to create the maximum variety of detail, at the same time preserving a strong underlying structure, if necessary employing rules, to hold the advertisement together. Assume for the purposes of this exercise only that the newspaper possesses whichever line composing faces (Linotype, Intertype and Ludlow) you happen to have typesheets for. An exercise such as this, though it may be thought aesthetically uninteresting, is most relevant to the practice of typography and is a searching test of the student's ability to organize and communicate.

Prepare a working layout for a three-column 8in advertisement to be trade-set and inserted in a popular national daily, the three-column measure totalling 32½ ems. The copy given is: 'Fly Spanair to South America/Leave London in the evening by one of the convenient connecting services via Frankfurt or Zurich and arrive next morning at Rio, Sao Paulo or Buenos Aires, or early afternoon at Santiago, with plenty of time to settle in or pick up a flight to another city. Ask your travel agent to book your next flight to South America by Spanair./Enjoy incomparable comfort, speed and service with Spanair/London/Manchester/Birmingham/Glasgow/Dublin'.

Although there is a definite information content, much of the purpose of this advertisement is to gain prestige. The success of the student's layout will depend greatly on how effectively it suggests to the reader those qualities which an international airline would wish to be part of its public image. The copy holds few clues as to style of presentation and the designer's preliminary analysis must therefore be more penetrating.

Often in an advertising campaign the typographer is required to adapt layouts with as little change as possible to new formats. When the above task has been completed, prepare a second layout closely resembling it, for the same kind of publication, single column of 10 ems 3pts, 10in deep.

151

Half-page advertisement for *The Times 500* appearing in *The Economist*

152

These differ from newspaper advertisements in that there is less intense competition on smaller pages, reading can generally be counted on to be more leisurely, and a magazine can expect a longer life than a newspaper. Its readership is often more precisely defined, and some periodicals in this class offer high quality paper and print, in black and colour. The direct and sometimes crude approach forced on the designer by the exigencies of newspaper advertising can here be modified, and in the correct place highly sophisticated work of considerable aesthetic worth may be attempted.

The following exercises are problems in the communication of very different ideas, in varied media, to groups of readers with differing tastes and expectations.

Prepare a working layout for a half-page advertisement 24 ems deep by 30 ems, no bleed possible, to be printed in black and a red-orange which is standard throughout the publication, on supercalendered stock in a brochure on family holidays at home and abroad. The copy supplied is : 'Have sun this summer/and soak up Jersey's unique blend of continental gaiety and home comforts. Enjoy water-skiing, skin-diving, underwater swimming and surfing. Miles of golden sand, sparkling blue sea, undiscovered bays. Your money goes further in Jersey, which offers you the best of both worlds. See for yourself this summer./Jersey/Send for free colour brochure to Department 146, States of Jersey Information Centre, Weigh-bridge, Jersey, CI'.

Advertisement in *Typographica*
for Grosvenor, Chater
printed black and russet

3 books 1 paper

For typographers, designers, and all those interested in the making of books, here are three recent books of outstanding quality.

Methods of Book Design
the practice of an industrial craft, by Hugh Williamson.
Published by Oxford University Press and printed at the University Press, Oxford, on Basingwerk Parchment.

A Suite of Fleurons
an enquiry into the history of printers' flowers, by John Ryder.
Published by Phoenix House Ltd and printed by Tinlings of Liverpool on Basingwerk Parchment.

By Request
an autobiography by André L. Simon.
Published by The Wine & Food Society and printed by The Curwen Press on Basingwerk Parchment.

Basingwerk Parchment
for fine book production.
Made by
Grosvenor, Chater & Co. Ltd
64 Cannon Street, London EC4
City 7141
and
Abbey Mills, Holywell
Flintshire.
TYPOGRAPHICA is also printed on Basingwerk Parchment.

Basingwerk Parchment

Make a working layout for a full-page advertisement, bleed optional, to be printed in black and one colour of choice, in a monthly magazine for engineers and architects, printed on coated stock, page size A4, type area 60 ems deep by 40 ems. Copy reads: 'A new angle on production problems/ Design with Argon Sections in mind/ 620 characters of text follow decribing the product: metal angle sections/ Argon Metal Products Limited/Irvine, Yorkshire/0904–12271/Also at London, Birmingham and St Helens, Lancs'.

Prepare a working layout for a quarter-page advertisement in a fashionable monthly magazine dealing with the life, landscape and culture of a particular region. Coated paper is used throughout and any one of the British Standard 3020 ink colours, already in use for the four-colour plates else-where in the publication, is to be used along with black. The area of the advertisement measures 27 ems deep by 22 ems, no bleed, and the copy is: 'Are you using the CoID's services?/ If you are a manufacturer the industrial division will consider your products for inclusion in our Design Index, a step towards inclusion in the Design Centre. If you want a designer the Centre can help you./If you are a journalist the Council's Press Office will help you to find out anything you want to know about design in Britain. If you are a retailer the retail section can give you a monthly list of new products on the Index./If you are a qualified designer the Record of Designers is a useful place to have your name and particulars noted./ Council of Industrial Design/Northern Committee/46 South Bridge Street, Newcastle'.

Quarter-page advertisement for Hely Thom in supplement to *Design* magazine

Contrast your finished work for this exercise with that of the second exercise in section 43. Each should be a successful essay in communication, but other-wise they represent near extremes in the contrasting demands made by content, readership, medium and printing techniques.

154

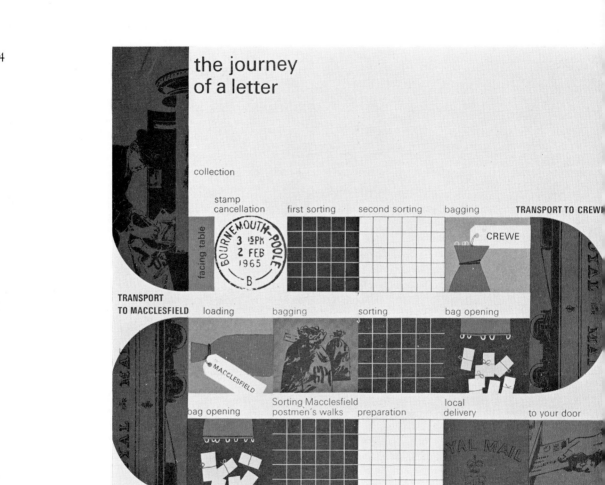

the journey
of a letter

collection

stamp
cancellation · first sorting · second sorting · bagging · TRANSPORT TO CREWE

facing table

TRANSPORT
TO MACCLESFIELD · loading · bagging · sorting · bag opening

bag opening · Sorting Macclesfield postmen's walks · preparation · local delivery · to your door

Pages from a G P O booklet
printed black, pink, orange and olive
showing in graphic form
the seven stages of a letter
*Reproduced by permission of
Her Majesty's Postmaster General*

45 graphic design

Correctly speaking, the term 'graphic design' encompasses the whole process of designing for printing, and should be further divided into typographic, autographic and photographic design. Typography, with which this book is concerned, deals with units which already exist in some form, be it metal or film. Autographic techniques are employed to make original images by drawing or its equivalent, requiring the camera to convert these into surfaces suitable for printing. This is also true of photographic images. However, graphic design or its abbreviation 'graphics' is commonly taken to mean the autographic part of design and should be understood in that sense here.

The former clear distinction between the three media has in any case become obscured in recent years by technological changes which make it easier to combine them. In particular, photolithography has removed the need for make-up in three dimensions. Closer integration of the three has become possible and this subject is taken up again in section 49.

While technical advances have made economically possible the great and continuing expansion of pictorial presentation in all kinds of print, the main impetus has come from public demand. Conditioned by among other things television and popular photography, people *expect* graphic methods of communication. According to McLuhan, notably in *The Gutenberg galaxy*, the implications of this social change are immense. Here it is enough to recognise that ideas conveyed through pictures, or by shape and colour alone, are different in kind from ideas capable of being expressed by the printed world.

The question for the designer becomes: at what point do typographic means alone become inadequate to perform efficiently the task of communication? There is no simple answer for all occasions but some guiding lines may be laid down.

In the first place, the resources of form, freed from the obligation to conform to the alphabet, are able to add enormously to the impact, expressiveness and attractiveness of print. The pictorial element, graphic or photographic, further stimulates interest and improves effectiveness. Especially in competitive print, it can be claimed that graphics and pictures increase its chances of being read, heighten its status and help it to communicate efficiently.

Secondly, as already mentioned, ideas which lend themselves to graphic presentation are not of the same class as are readily conveyed by written language. In everyday use words are fairly factual and precise, their meanings clearly defined. Images are much more open to varied interpretation but can also be made to carry more emotional overtones. This is admittedly a gross

45

oversimplification but it is nonetheless true that when persuasion rather than information is the purpose of the piece of print, graphics and pictures are called for.

The usefulness of graphic techniques in other ways must not be overlooked. The superiority of pictorial representation of objects and scenes over verbal

Brochure cover
printed yellow, orange and black
for Scottish opera

Political leaflet
printed in brown
for Scottish
Nationalist Party

description is obvious. There are many instances where pictures are more detailed and specific than words, for example in instructional pamphlets. The social significance of this is pointed out in an important book by Ivins: *Prints and visual communication*.

Graphic symbolism, as in signs, maps, graphs and diagrams, is a field capable of being more thoroughly exploited. Certain kinds of information are more quickly and easily understood when coded in this way. The important book by Bowman: *Graphic communication*, explores this field in great depth.

Finally, shape and colour on their own, without direct assistance from pictorial representation, are able to communicate ideas. This is the principle behind abstraction in art and provides the graphic designer with a powerful

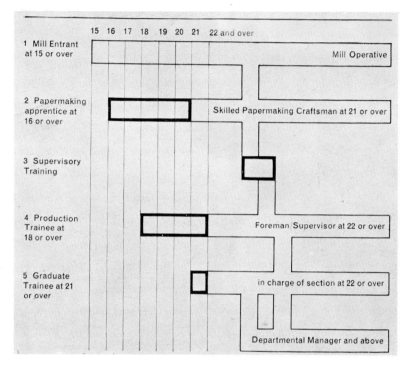

Diagram of training schemes
from a booklet
issued by Wiggins Teape

language of expression, though it may be that public sensitivity to the qualities of pure form is as yet less than is sometimes assumed. It should go without saying that in designing print self-expression is very subordinate to the task of reinforcing the message of the text by the use of this visual language.

It is evident that autographic and photographic methods of communication in print are likely in the future to become even more widely employed and their techniques enlarged. The student has probably experienced for himself the limitations imposed on him by the typographic terms of the last exercises and instinctively felt the need to introduce graphics. However, it cannot be within the scope of this volume to deal with such an extensive subject. For the specialist typographer it is in any case enough that he should have some insight into other media, so that he can work effectively along with a graphic designer and photographer.

Graphic design today shares with typography its historical background—the modern movement in art and the applied arts, with special reference to the innovations of the Bauhaus. At this famous school the influence of the experimental methods and ways of thinking of twentieth-century science and

45

Jackson Nelson's **Annual Dinner Dance** will be held in the Burnside Hotel Rutherglen
Friday 22 December 1967 at 7 30 for 8 00 until 1 a m Transport available Dress optional

Dance ticket
printed silver and red
on cast-coated

technology led to the adoption of a training system which sought to study and analyse the visual aspects of experience. More recently, the findings of perception psychologists have been introduced to give this study a more scientific basis (see Scott: *Design fundamentals*). Basic design, as this approach has come to be called, is not a catalogue of ready-made solutions to design problems, still less a fashionable style, but simply a series of investigations into the expressive nature of form and colour, aimed at teaching the vocabulary and the grammar of the visual language. Some useful books will be found in the bibliography.

Basic design is important to the typographer too, though hardly ever can he use form for its own sake: the words come first. Whenever formal relationships are of value in a layout, an appreciation of the factors influencing them is essential. It is hoped that those parts of basic design which particularly apply to typography will be found to have been covered in this book, without the need for specific exercises in abstract shapes and colours, which can so easily mislead the student typographer.

Methods of reproducing graphic and photographic work must not be neglected and in Biggs: *Illustration and reproduction*, Croy: *Graphic design and reproduction techniques*, Cannon & Wallis: *Graphic reproduction* and Curwen: *Processes of graphic reproduction* much information on this subject can be found.

Making a unity from varied typographic material is not easy, but when an 159 illustration or symbol is also to be integrated the task is more difficult still. The aim must be to weld everything together in such a way that the reader has the impression that the same creative impulse is at work throughout.

In the majority of cases, the graphics are given first consideration and the typographer is faced with the problem of adding typography to artwork which has already been drawn. He must begin by closely studying this artwork and assessing certain of its main qualities: mass, form, direction, tonal value and style. Let us look at each in turn.

The mass of an illustration or symbol is a result of its area and tonal value. The bigger and darker it is, in other words, the greater is its mass and the

Exhibition announcement
by Letraset
printed red and black
and
magazine advertisement
for Charles Morgan
printed red and black

GRAPHIC STUDENT AWARDS

Presented by Letraset Ltd
You are invited to an exhibition
of the award winning designs
together with a selection of other entries
October 3 – 14 : 10 a.m. to 7 p.m.
Thursdays 8.30 p.m. Saturday 1 p.m.
Admission free
Ceylon Tea Centre
22, Regent Street (Piccadilly Circus)
London W.1

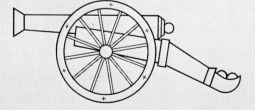

Charles Morgan & Co Ltd
Casa Fundada en 1760
Durante más de 200 años
venimos suministrando
nuestros productos a
impresores y papeleros
de toda el mundo con
entera satisfaccion de los
consumidores
¿Aprovecha Vd. nuestra
experiencia de más de
200 años?

Studio Vista letterheading
printed black and ochre

Studio Vista Limited publishers

Blue Star House, Highgate Hill, London N.19

Telephone/01-272 7531
Telegrams/Studiopub London N.19

160

more dominating it appears within the layout. A principle introduced earlier was the desirability of having a single dominant feature in any design, round which the other elements can be organised. When type and graphics are combined, it must be decided which is more important and which subsidiary. In most cases the greater interest evoked by an illustration is the decisive factor in its favour, as in figs. 1, 3, 4, 5, 6 and 7, but relative mass must also be taken into account. Should the type mass be very much more, it may be better to allow the main line to dominate the layout, as it does in fig. 2.

The purpose of the printed job has also to be considered. For example, when a symbol appears on a letterheading the firm's name may be reduced to a point size only slightly greater than the rest of the copy, because its function as a recognition feature has been usurped by the symbol, as has occurred in fig. 3. The main type line must not compete for attention with the symbol. In all the figures shown here, note the importance of balancing type mass against the mass of the graphic element.

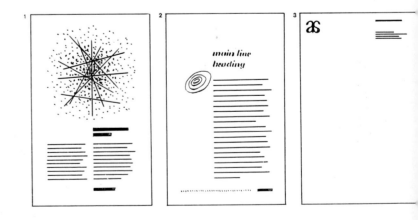

The shape of the illustration or symbol is the next feature of importance to integration. The outline is a form which must be included within the composition. When this outline is rectangular, not much difficulty is likely to be experienced in relating its horizontals and verticals to a grid, as can be seen in fig. 4, but curved and irregular shapes may require careful handling. In many cases the internal lines of composition of the illustration prove useful, as in fig. 5. Many symbols are symmetrical in conception and should not be forced into arbitrary asymmetric positions. But look at fig. 5 for a successful amalgam of centred and asymmetric.

Both outline shape and the actual subject of illustrations can be directional: that is, they may give the impression of facing one way rather than another, and impelling the reader's attention in that direction. Certain shapes, typified most vividly by the arrow, point in one direction. Objects such as cars, pencils and chairs have a front and back and point forward. The most powerful manifestation of this is when the human face is illustrated: the reader follows the direction of its gaze. Graphics possessing definite directional properties should face into the page rather than out of it, and main lines placed in their paths will gain in emphasis. (fig. 7).

The conventions of reading from left to right and from top to bottom affect the way we look at the printed page. The eye enters top left and scans the page in a clockwise direction. Pictures with directional tendencies and accompanying type should be placed accordingly and should not try to force the eye to travel in unnatural ways. Once the initial quick look has been taken, however, the reader's attention may wander in any direction. A good layout establishes in his mind at first glance the extent of the information, its organization, the relative importance of the various groups and the relationships between them. He is then at liberty to choose where his interest lies.

Tonal value is the overall impression of lightness or darkness of an area. Until now our concern has been with lines and masses of type, but illustrations also can be said to be light or dark in overall terms, though they may present

Highway code cover
printed dark green
blue and yellow
*Reproduced by permission
of Ministry of Transport*
and a Penguin Books showcard
printed orange and black

a less even texture. Even when reproduced by line process, thickness of line and number of lines to the area contribute to a tonal effect. A satisfactor relationship between the tonal values of graphics and type must be found within a page.

The harmony created by matching closely the tonal appearance of the tw can be very pleasing, as in fig. 5, but more often a contrast is sought, partic ularly in contemporary design. Where pronounced contrast between light an dark is present in the subject of the illustration, or the form of the graphic it may be echoed in a similar tonal contrast between main lines and text, as i figs. 1 and 4. Artwork which consists of continuous tones, such as a was drawing, is better considered along with photographs in the following section

While mass, shape, direction and tonal value can be appreciated as visua facts, style is less easy to define. The medium used, whether pen, brus scraperboard or whatever, imparts a certain character, which can be matche typographically. For example, modern types share the characteristics of fin pen drawings and engravings, while strictly geometric artwork using drawin instruments combines well with sanserif. But the essential ingredient of styl is the personal manner of drawing of the artist himself. A sympathy must b established with this before it is possible to create typography which will shar that style. The object is still to make a unified design where there is no in congruity, no conflict of styles. It should never be apparent that more tha one person has contributed to the final result, and this is the responsibility the typographer.

repare a working layout for a letter-
eading and compliments slip, to be
rinted in two workings, copy being:
Charles Munroe Limited/Seed
herchants/133 Lesser Barrow Street,
aichester/Telephone, 0793–2456'.
Give full details of paper and ink. This
ymbol is to be incorporated in both
obs, in any suitable size and
olour(s).

Further practice in integrating graphics and type should be carried out by the student, using line artwork cut from magazines, especially in the advertising field. Copy, space and specification may be the same as in the existing print, but a completely new layout should be made.

Redesigning a job is more difficult than working from client's copy, because the original communication problem must first be rediscovered before progress can be made towards a satisfactory design solution which ignores the previous layout. Writing out the copy again is a good practice. Look for good artwork poorly combined with typography when choosing redesigning exercises.

163

Publisher's
advertising leaflet
by Pitman
printed black
and tan

47 photography

As techniques based on photography become increasingly employed in production stages preparatory to printing, they also become the logical way of creating images. Photocomposition and photolettering devices are such methods applied to typography, while apart from straightforward photography, the camera is today much in demand to produce images which are non-representational. A good basic guide to camera techniques can be found in Croy: *Graphic design and reproduction techniques*, while some of the special techniques available to extend the scope of photography in the direction of graphics can be seen in Croy: *Design in photography* and *Creative photography*. Here, however, we are concerned only with conventional photographs.

The camera offers several advantages over its graphic equivalent of drawn illustration. The detail in a good photograph is inexhaustible and not subject to the personal interpretation of the artist. When the subject is complex, it is often quicker and cheaper. A photograph is also more convincing than a drawing, because it is popularly if erroneously held that 'the camera cannot lie'.

On the other hand, an artist can be more selective and therefore more relevant in his depiction of detail. He can flatter and persuade in a way difficult for the camera. In short, the choice between artist and photographer depends on the nature of the job in hand—they are not equivalent to each other. Those particularly interested in the problem are invited to read Ivins: *Prints and visual communication*.

Like graphic design, the photograph is potentially a good eye-catching device and therefore extremely useful in competitive print. It stimulates the reader's interest almost entirely through its content, unlike artwork which also communicates powerfully through style and its formal properties. The positioning of pictures on the page and in relation to accompanying wording has come in for a certain amount of experimental investigation, with fairly predictable results. The larger the picture, the more effective it is; unusual proportions stimulate interest; high positions on the page, preceding the text, work best. Remember, however, the value of novelty in competitive print.

The typographer is often responsible for cropping (trimming) of photographs and their presentation for reproduction. Cropping is nearly always desirable, because the format of a photographic print is decided by film size instead of subject, leading to the inclusion of unwanted detail and uninteresting areas around the edges. A knowledge of composition derived from basic design exercises is essential if an interesting, complete and balanced picture is to emerge. A chapter on this aspect is contained in Wills: *Fundamentals of layout.*

Suitability of print quality for reproduction, together with matters of screen and scaling, are fully dealt with in Cannon & Wallis: *Graphic reproduction.*

Though not within the scope of this book, an awareness of the possibilities, technical and creative, of photography and the photographic processes practised in the printing industry is vital to the expert typographer, who may be asked to commission photographs. A number of useful books are in print and the reader's attention is particularly drawn to Baker: *Visual persuasion.*

Studio set-up
for the photograph on p. 11
showing original sketch
and trial polaroid print

166

The problems of integrating photographs into a layout are similar to those encountered in section 46 in relation to graphics. The outline shape of a photographic print is often rectangular ('squared-up') and is therefore easily accommodated within a grid. Internally, the compositional lines of the picture are again useful for projecting axes and lining type, where such structural lines are obvious to the eye as in the illustration under.

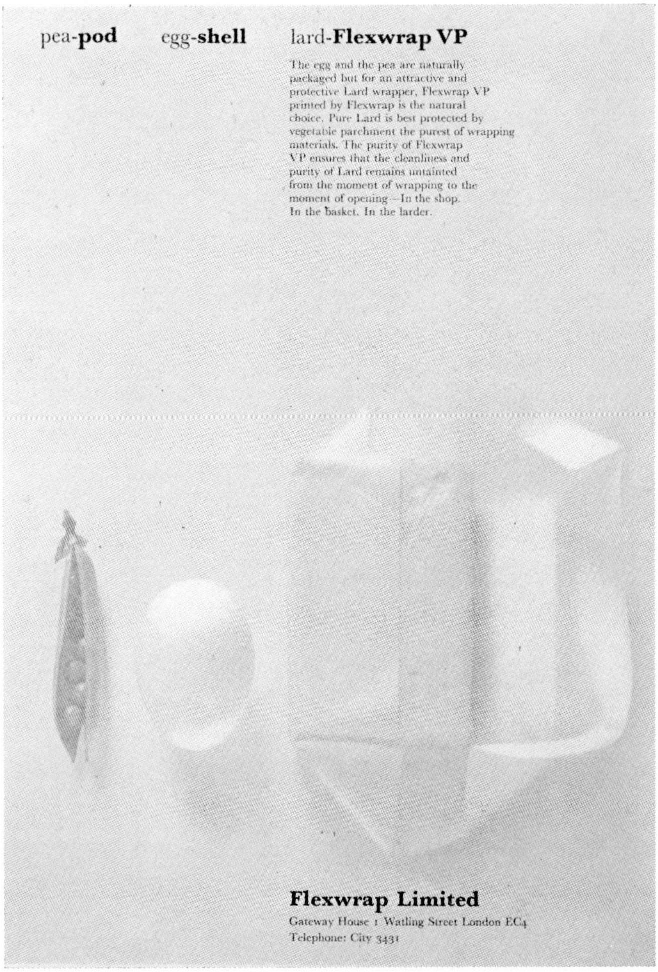

Magazine advertisement
for Flexwrap
printed black
on blue

pea-**pod**   egg-**shell**   lard-**Flexwrap VP**

The egg and the pea are naturally packaged but for an attractive and protective Lard wrapper, Flexwrap VP printed by Flexwrap is the natural choice. Pure Lard is best protected by vegetable parchment the purest of wrapping materials. The purity of Flexwrap VP ensures that the cleanliness and purity of Lard remains untainted from the moment of wrapping to the moment of opening—In the shop. In the basket. In the larder.

Flexwrap Limited
Gateway House 1 Watling Street London EC4
Telephone: City 3431

The feeling of direction is strong in many photographs and then dictates the placing of accompanying type, as in the next illustration.

SCOTTISH DESIGN CENTRE

RIGHT
FOR THE
JOB

An Omega does more for you than tell the time.

Read the fifth part of a second with the new Chronostop by Omega

Omega, official timekeeper for the 1968 Olympic Games, has created this modern stop-second watch for those who want to capture time on the run.
The Chronostop is an elegant everyday watch in stainless steel. It has luminous markers, coloured hands, charcoal grey dial and a choice of leather or metal bracelet. It is waterproof, shock protected and anti-magnetic. Come in and try on a Chronostop. It costs only £29.10.0. Ω
OMEGA

Folder for
Scottish Design Centre
and
press advertisement
for Omega

A photograph is composed of continuous tones, setting problems in its tonal integration with typography, but in practice it is the overall impression which counts: whether it is high-key as in the example on page 166, or low-key as above right, and also whether there is a great deal of contrast within the picture between lights and darks, or very little. The more limited tonal resources of type can nonetheless be made to echo or alternatively contrast with the tonal qualities of the photograph. Study all the illustrations in this section.

In illustrated print, coated stock is preferred to give life and detail to half-tones, particularly in letterpress. Text types which print well on coated papers are few and to this limitation is now added the desirability of stylistic harmony with the photograph. In a way this is easier to achieve than with graphics, because with the camera there is less direct personal involvement. Sanserif, which alone has the range of weights to match photography's tones, is also much the best choice stylistically, but type selection must ultimately depend on the nature of the individual job.

The satisfactory positioning of an illustration on the page involves a number of factors in addition to those mentioned in the previous section. Such a placing constitutes a major division of the area and the laws concerning the creation of axes apply, as can be seen in the illustrations. Picture content and direction suggest whether a top, foot or side position would be most suitable.

The practice of bleeding half-tones is today common and can be justified in certain contexts. Removal of some or all of the marginal space simplifies and increases the apparent size and the impact of an illustrated page. If the layout is already lacking in interesting detail, this may make it duller still though. An occasional judicious bled edge, contrasted with other edges which have been allowed to retain their marginal space, is an additional source of variety for the designer, but should not be abused.

Margins seem to encourage the illusion of there being two planes to the printed sheet: the paper surface in the background and a nearer, superimposed

Cover of a booklet
for Glaxo
printed full colour
and grey

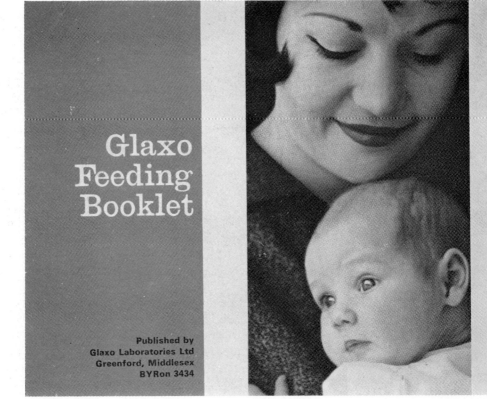

Glaxo
Feeding
Booklet

Published by
Glaxo Laboratories Ltd
Greenford, Middlesex
BYRon 3434

plane consisting of the inked image. The elimination of margins by bleeding rules and illustrations reduces this illusion, the ensuing flatness taking on more of the quality of a two-dimensional pattern. Sanserif types also have this effect, which is capable of being used to advantage, but may also produce a dead, monotonous appearance.

Bleed on a left-hand foredge or top, especially if accompanied by unusual and arbitrary cropping of the subject, affords an effectively dramatic lead-in for the eye. The same device applied to the right-hand foredge, as was discovered with rules in section 27, causes the reader to expect a continuation overleaf. This is of value only on a cover, and occasionally in spreads in multi-page work.

Full-colour photographs add the problem of colour to that of tonal relationships with typography. It is advisable to continue to treat the situation as one of tonal values, printing the type in black. Half-closing the eyes translates the colours in the photograph into tones for the purpose of matching them typographically. Alternatively, an important but small unit of type can be put in colour, matching exactly or forming a harmony with some similarly small

Fold-out leaflet
for Triplex
printed black and green

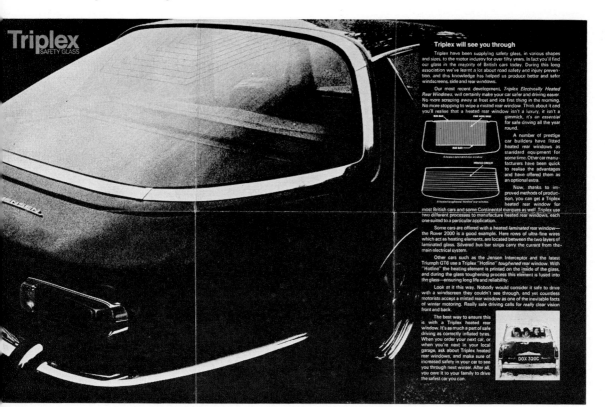

but important patch of colour in the picture. To do this satisfactorily entails the expense of a fifth printing, because the available standard cyan or magenta is very rarely appropriate.

Keep in mind while preparing layouts for all work which combines type with half-tones that, if the illustration dominates, as it does on most occasions, it attracts the reader's attention first. The main type lines should be close enough, and in the proper position, to be read while his eye is scanning the picture. The remaining text should not imply unnatural movements of the eye. The whole typographic treatment should again aim at simplicity, leaving the illustration to focus attention and stimulate interest.

Prepare a working layout for a page, printed black and one colour on coated stock, for insertion in a loose-leaf folder. The layout is to be standard to a series of pages giving information to architects on a range of related building materials. On each page a photograph, to be scaled down from original prints all 4in deep by 5in, all low key with dramatic lighting, is to be included. Copy comprises a heading not exceeding six words, followed by a maximum of 400 words text (multiply words by six to convert to characters). A table with six equal columns, each containing up to three figures, and eight lines in depth is also to be included. At the head of the page the month and year should appear, while at the foot the firm's name and address is to be displayed. The recommendations for form and layout contained in *The preparation of trade literature for the building industry* must be adhered to, and an SfB/UDC reference box is essential.

170

Exhibition catalogue cover
printed black

49 printing processes

At the beginning of this book it was said that some acquaintance with the principles, skills and processes of letterpress printing was demanded of the student. All exercises have since been based on the assumption that this method of printing was to be employed. Now some knowledge of alternative printing processes is needed, to find out in what ways they affect the technical feasibility, cost and appearance of a design. Descriptions of letterpress, lithography, photogravure and screen printing are given in chapters 6 to 8 of Clowes: *A guide to printing* and can be supplemented by reference to other books. The only purpose here is to examine the bearing the process might have on typographic design.

For the printing of type, letterpress is almost the ideal method, the characteristic impression on the paper being sharp and dense. Most typefaces are in fact designed to look their best when printed letterpress on uncoated paper. Line illustrations too have this definition, though very fine detail needs a smooth-surfaced stock. A disadvantage of the process is that half-tones of fine screen cannot be printed successfully on uncoated paper, but as it is possible to adjust local impression on the printing machine, there tends to be more contrast between highlights and shadow areas. As blocks and type matter are produced separately, then combined into pages in their three-dimensional forms, integration of the two is less complete than is the case with those processes where photography is used.

Of the rival processes to letterpress, lithography is the most widely used and most versatile. Almost any of the exercises completed by the student to date could have been produced equally well, though not necessarily at the same cost, by lithography. The type, set as for letterpress, but not perhaps made up into pages, would have been carefully proofed on a suitable coated paper and then assembled and photographed to make a negative or positive for transferring to the printing plate.

Alternative methods of typesetting for lithography are by special electric typewriter, which produces justified or unjustified lines of text in a limited number of alphabets of a face perhaps only slightly inferior to conventionally set romans; and by photocomposition, whose end product is negative or positive film, thus eliminating the camera stage. Text by typewriter is cheap but not of high quality, though adequate for medium-quality work, while that of photocomposition is often as expensive as hot-metal type but offers a very high-quality image.

Specifications on working layouts for the most widely-used system of photosetting, the Monophoto, are worded slightly differently, as outlined in

Monotype Newsletter, volume XLIII, number 2: *Filmsetting in focus.*

An advantage of filmsetting is that the range of type sizes is greatly increased, since all sizes are obtained by photographic enlargement of two or so basic founts. Unfortunately, this sometimes causes a perceptible coarsening in the appearance of larger types (with metal type, a different drawing is made for each major point size). As corrections and complicated make-up in film are expensive, thorough preparation of copy and accurate layout are more than ever essential.

In the reproduction of illustrations lithography has a number of advantages. Unlike letterpress half-tones, which require a coarser screen when the stock is uncoated, fine screens can be printed on a wide variety of surfaces, though coateds are still preferred for the most brilliant results. Separate handling of type and plates, together with the exigences of their assembly, are constricting factors in letterpress. The separation is not so complete in lithography, enabling closer integration of type, photographs and graphics. Reversals, cut-out, deep-etch and vignette finishes are more easily obtained and more use can therefore be made of them.

The nature of lithography is such that a thinner film of ink is transferred to the paper than is the case with letterpress. In the finest machining this is hardly noticeable, as lithographic inks are highly concentrated in pigment, but in everyday commercial work blacks may look insufficiently dense and colours lack intensity. The choice of a high white stock minimizes this. On the other hand, an advantage is held by lithography in its ability to print large flat areas on relatively rough surfaces. Such solids, with or without reversed line, are simple to specify and easy to make at the film stage, and the creative possibilities are great.

A slight sharpening, or more often thickening of type image sometimes takes place, affecting the character of text matter particularly. The difficulty is discussed in Dowding: *Factors in the choice of typefaces.*

The typographer is hardly ever asked to design for photogravure, which for economic reasons specializes in very long runs of illustrated magazines, packaging and similar work. All the remarks about photolithography apply equally to gravure, with the added information that this process best gives the illusion of continuous tones and renders colour most faithfully. But see Dowding's book for its effect on type.

Screen printing is a short-run process without the fineness of detail obtained by the other three main printing methods. Type in text sizes and all but the extremely coarse half-tone screens used in street posters are not recommended for reproduction by screen process.

An important advantage is that totally opaque inks, matt or gloss, can be deposited in a very thick film, enabling light colours to be successfully overprinted on dark—even white on top of black. Posters and showcards are given great impact and appeal by the intensity of screen inks, which may be printed on an extraordinarily wide range of materials and surfaces. Stencils are made photographically, therefore artwork and type pulls can be mounted in position by the designer, ready for the camera. Simple shapes may be cut by hand by the printer, lowering the cost.

Further familiarity with the effects characteristic of the various printing processes, with knowledge of their limitations and relative costs, can be gained only through long experience of designing for them. This survey, it should be understood, does no more than provide a guide to several of their basic features, while certain other points arise in the final section.

Pages from a booklet
for National Benzole
filmset in Monophoto Baskerville
colour separations of paintings
by electronic scanner
printed offset lithography
on cartridge

Runswick Bay, Yorkshire

Cottage Gardens

Week-end cottage gardens have cocktail patios and labour-saving evergreens. Old miners' and weavers' cottage gardens grew food, auriculas and picotees. To these rather functional domains we prefer the 'sampler' type of cottage garden, the labourer's plot, not vastly changed from the days when it was half a man's livelihood and all of his recreation. Such gardens still harbour vanishing flowers, still care little about 'one-season' planting or problems concerning vistas and relative proportions.

Once the cabbages and marrows and so on are accommodated, there is a casually supervised free-for-all, a jumble-sale drifting and banking of tufts and cushions, climbers and clingers, with bees revelling, warring scents besieging the kitchen, and kittens wrestling among the lavenders.

Pinks with bursting bodices line brick paths; wallflowers both native copper and strident Siberian gold dispute every inch with hollyhocks, lilies, foxgloves, tobacco-plants, dovecote, wellhead and mangle. Stonecrop and valerian claim the walltops, Old China and Maiden's Blush roses the palings, orange and mustard lichens the roof. Somehow or other, forgotten appletrees, Morgan Sweets and Quarrendens, find rootroom among the rhubarb.

Ideally, everything is copious, colourful, askew . . . or, if it is not, it soon will be, as soon as you turn your back for a week or so.

Wisborough Green, Sussex

50 cost effectiveness

The aim of the designer of print is to ensure its maximum effectiveness for the least expenditure. This is not the same as saying that all work should be produced cheaply; many jobs demand expensive production in order to fulfil their functions properly.

Throughout this book the reader has been constantly reminded that every design decision is governed to some extent by cost, and has been given the information needed to avoid incurring unnecessary expense through misuse of the materials, techniques and equipment of the printing trade. In this last section we look more broadly at the whole question of value for money.

The price charged by the printer for producing a given job is made up of the cost of materials and labour expended, plus his profit. Paper is usually the biggest item among materials and from the data given in sections 28 and 37 it should be possible for the student to arrive at a fairly accurate estimate of its total cost. Ink is a significant charge only in the case of screen printing where large solid printed areas noticeably increase the cost.

The prices of letterpress line and half-tone plates are available on request from any process engraver. Note that the scale of charges rises with size, but that all plates up to a certain area are charged at a minimum figure. It is sometimes possible to mount together different pieces of artwork, undergoing the same reduction, to keep down expense. When a large number of illustrations appear throughout a job, it may be cheaper to print by lithography. The printer in this process makes his own negatives, line and screened, transferring everything at the same time to the printing plate, so cost comparisons often show a saving to be made. It may be possible at the same time to make further economies by specifying an uncoated paper.

When it comes to typesetting, the additional stages of making type pulls for reproduction, photographing and platemaking make the initial expense incurred with lithography greater than with letterpress, which prints directly from the same type. Filmsetting, for an account of which see chapter 3 of Clowes: *A guide to printing*, narrows the difference when available. Film make-up is more flexible than its three-dimensional counterpart, and complex make-up simpler and cheaper. The use of filmsetting almost certainly implies lithographic printing, though it is possible to make relief plates to print letterpress.

The typographer's work is not finished with the preparation of layouts and specification data. Proofs have to be checked for accurate following of the layout by the printer and minor details improved. The correction of the wording is the responsibility of the client. Rough page proofs are included in the printer's estimated price, while galley proofs for pasting up into a dummy—an excellent practice in book and other multi-page work—are supplied for very little extra. Additional proofs, author's corrections beyond the normal and machine proofs in colour, up to finished standard, are charged separately. The last is a very expensive item indeed and only when the appearance of a job is extremely important to its effectiveness and the total cash involved amounts to a large sum, are machine proofs economically justified.

Letterpress machining offers easy alteration of the forme right up to and during the run, which is not possible without making a new printing surface in any of the alternative processes. In general, however, running speeds tend to be slower than in lithography and gravure, making long runs less competitive in price. Presses which print several colours at the same time are commoner in the other two processes, giving them an economic advantage in colour work.

It can therefore be concluded that length of run, cost of preparing printing surfaces, and amount of colour and illustration present are some of the main factors in selecting the most economic printing method. But as the appearance of the job is also affected to some degree by the process used, cost cannot be made the sole criterion. Effectiveness and quality must be taken into account and a compromise reached between them and cost if a conflict occurs. As an instance of this, it is possible to quote the case of screen printing, which being only semi-automatic is comparatively dear for long runs, but offers effects which are unobtainable by any other means.

Finishing processes such as creasing, folding, stitching and trimming must be allowed for in any estimate of the final cost. A percentage of the total is then added as profit and purchase tax listed where it applies.

From all this it will be realised that the first essentials for economic production are correct and well marked-up copy, an accurate working layout and a specification for production which takes into consideration all relevant factors. Only if these requirements are complied with will our original aim of maximum effectiveness for the least cost be capable of achievement.

The proportion of total outlay spent on any one item is a particular concern of the designer. If, for example, the amount of paper used is large, quite a small decrease in price per pound has a significant effect on cost. Conversely, if the main expense falls elsewhere, it may make little difference to the total cost if a very good quality paper is chosen, with beneficial effect to the appearance of the job. Typesetting, especially by hand, is always expensive and in small run work accounts for much of the cost. In this kind of work economies must be made wherever possible, on the lines laid down throughout this book. When a large number of copies is wanted, unit cost is lowered and typesetting, together with other initial expenditure, becomes proportionately less of the total sum, whereupon it becomes less important to make strict economies that will reduce the effectiveness of the print.

Design costs are a matter for the individual firm or designer, to which are added fees for artwork and photographs. The preparation of a finished layout for customer submission and approval reduces the risk of committing him to expense without his knowing whether the resultant job is likely to be satisfactory to him or not. Major alterations must be carried out at this stage, never after the proof has been received, when changes are prohibitively expensive. The finished layout has few other uses, however, and as it is costly to prepare its usefulness must be weighed against how much it adds to initial costs.

The British Federation of Master Printers' *Estimating for printers* contains much valuable information on the subject of costs in the printing industry and should be consulted when detailed coverage of any aspect of printing economics is sought.

books to read

This list of titles is reasonably comprehensive but is not to be taken as exhaustive. That a book does not appear below does not necessarily mean that it cannot be recommended. As far as possible books still in print at time of writing have been preferred, but when, as in a few instances, the title is known to be out of print, this fact is stated. A brief description of the content of each book is appended, to enable the reader to pursue his particular interests. Few of the many titles on lettering and type design have been listed.

ANDERSON *Elements of design* (Holt, Rinehart & Winston, New York). An outstanding theoretical survey of graphic design in its widest sense, aptly illustrated.

BANHAM *Theory and design in the first machine age* (Architectural Press). Classic work on the modern movement. Though mainly concerned with architecture, necessary reading to anyone who wishes to understand the thinking behind the development of modern design in any field. Should be read in conjunction with Pevsner below.

BAKER *Advertising layout and art direction* (McGraw-Hill). Contains much sound advice on the hard facts of advertising layout.

BAKER *Visual persuasion* (McGraw-Hill). Expert instruction in the use of photography in advertising.

BAYNES *Industrial design and the community* (Lund Humphries). Defines neatly the relationship between the designer and society and presents some valuable case histories of design projects.

BIGGS *An approach to type* (Blandford). Contains information essential to the beginner's understanding of the nature of type and its forms. Read particularly the chapter on legibility.

BIGGS *Basic typography* (Faber). One of the few really essential books on the subject. Deals with the principles of type design and setting, with particularly well-presented information on printing processes.

BIGGS *Illustration and reproduction* (Blandford). The autographic and printing processes explained and illustrated.

BIGGS *The craft of lettering* (Blandford). Basic roman letterforms. A number of equally fine books on this subject exist but are not listed here.

BIGGS *The use of type* (Blandford). Important preliminary reading to the present work.

BOWMAN *Graphic communication* (Wiley, New York). Explores in depth the language of graphics from the point of view of the theory of communications: graphs, diagrams etc.

BRADSHAW *Design* (Studio Vista). Highly readable advice and information for the designer of print.

BURNS *Typography* (Reinhold). An interesting book for the experienced designer or advanced student only.

BURT *A psychological study of typography* (Cambridge). Though written some time ago, still a good brief introtuion to the legibility problem. See Zachrisson for a more recent and extensive study.

CANNON, WALLIS *Graphic reproduction* (Studio Vista). A complete basic guide to the subject, indispensable to the print designer for study and reference.

CLOWES *A guide to printing* (Heinemann). Description of the main processes and printing techniques for the beginner.

COOKE *Colour by overprinting* (Winston, Philadelphia). Useful reference work, extensively illustrated in colour, for designers using this technique.

CORBUSIER *The modular* (Faber). Discloses some of the reasoning which has led to a renewed interest in the mathematics of good proportion.

CROY, O.R. *Design by photography* (Focal Press). Invaluable survey of advanced photographic techniques, fully illustrated and with practical instructions. A companion volume, *Creative photography*, by the same author and publisher, extends the field.

CROY, P. *Graphic design and reproduction techniques* (Focal Press). Contains a great deal of information on all aspects of designing for print. Especially useful on printing processes, graphics and photography.

CURWEN *Processes of graphic reproduction* (Faber). Similar in scope to Biggs' work.

DAIR *Design with type* (Benn). Excellent theoretic study of typography, more interesting to the experienced designer or advanced student. It would be a good idea to read it after the present work.

DAY *The typography of press advertisement* (Benn). A thorough study, though as is only to be expected in this field, some examples have dated.

DOWDING *Factors in the choice of type faces* (Wace). This exhaustive and authoritative essay is essential reading.

DOWDING *Finer points in the spacing and arrangement of type* (Wace). A thorough knowledge of this book is required before commencing the present work.

DOWDING *The history of printing types* (Wace). Readable, comprehensive and well-illustrated account of an overwritten subject.

EKSALL *Corporate design programs* (Studio Vista). Outlines the thinking behind the creation of a comprehensive house style, based on constructivist principles.

FYFFE *Basic copyfitting* (Studio Vista). Should be in the possession of all who design for print.

GARLAND *Graphics handbook* (Studio Vista). Typifies the up-to-date approach to graphic design.

GHYKA *Geometric composition and design* (Tiranti). For those who wish to know more about the mathematics of good proportion in the division of area.

GREEN *Creative print making* and *Introducing surface printing* (Batsford). Ideas for imaginative exercises in basic design with a special relevance to printing.

GROPIUS *The new architecture and the Bauhaus* (Faber). A short account of the ideas and practice of the famous school of design by its director, still relevant today and vital to an understanding of the modern movment.

HENRION, PARKIN *Design co-ordination and corporate image* (Studio Vista). An authoritative examination of the problems met with in formulating a house style, with many examples of their successful solution by top designers.

HOFMANN *Graphic design manual* (Tiranti). Basic course of the Swiss school of graphic design, with implications for the typographer.

HUTCHINS *Typographics* (Studio Vista). Technical information for designers, handy for reading or reference.

HUTT *Newspaper design* (Oxford). The definitive work on the subject, it makes useful background reading to the design of press advertisements.

ITTEN *The art of colour* (Reinhold, New York). Probably the most interesting work on the theory of colour from the artist's viewpoint, though very expensive. See also Renner.

IVINS *Prints and visual communication* (Routledge). A vital book for anyone interested in the nature of pictorial communication.

LAWLEY A basic course in art (Lund Humphries). A practical introduction to basic design.

LEE *Bookmaking* (Bowler, New York). More than a detailed guide to the design and production of books, it should be closely studied by any typographer who wishes to know more about the design and production of all kinds of print.

LEWIS *A handbook of type and illustration* (Faber). Similar, but not identical in scope to the works by Biggs and Curwen in the field of illustration, and with additional sections on type usage.

LEWIS *Typography, basic principles* (Studio Vista). Sound advice on various aspects by a well-known designer, with a particularly interesting chapter on the evolution of contemporary style.

LEWIS, BRINKLEY *Graphic design* (Routledge). Excellent historical survey of graphic design and typography with chapters on the place of the designer today.

LOCKWOOD *Diagrams* (Studio Vista). A comprehensive guide to the problems of effective communication of information by the use of graphic techniques.

MAURELLO *How to do paste-ups and mechanicals* (Tudor, New York). Helpful practical guide to the preparation of artwork, photographs, type and lettering for the process camera.

MCLEAN *Magazine design* (Oxford). A unique illustrated survey of the field with critical comment.

MCLUHAN *The Gutenberg galaxy* (Routledge) and *Understanding media* (Sphere). Not recommended reading for any but those interested particularly in the wider aspects of communication, though the same author's *The medium is the message* (Penguin) gives the gist of his argument in popular form.

MOHOLY-NAGY *Painting, photography, film* (Lund Humphries). Reprint of a Bauhaus book by this most original and influential figure.

MORISON *First principles of typography* (Cambridge). A booklet which is the classic statement of the nature of typography.

MORISON *The typographic arts* (Sylvan Press) out of print. Scholarly essays on the nature of typography which are compulsory reading.

MORISON *Type designs, past and present* (Benn). Short masterly account of the development of text typeface design. For a fuller study see the same author's *Letter forms*.

MÜLLER-BROCKMANN *The graphic artist and his design problem* (Tiranti). Well-illustrated statement of the fashionable Swiss approach to graphic and typographic design.

MURGATROYD *Modern graphics* (Studio Vista). Stimulating illustrated account of the most advanced international graphics.

NAYLOR *The Bauhaus* (Studio Vista). An historical appraisal of this famous design school.

NESBITT *The history and technique of lettering* (Dover, New York). A very complete treatment of the subject.

PEVSNER *Pioneers of modern design* (Penguin). This classic work should be read in conjunction with Banham on the same subject.

POTTER *What is a designer?* A perceptive essay on the training, methods of working and values of designers.

PYE *The nature of design* (Studio Vista). A readable book on design philosophy.

READ *Art and industry* (Faber). An inquiry into the philosophy of industrial design.

RENNER *Colour order and harmony* (Studio Vista). On similar lines to Itten, but much less expensively produced.

ROBERTS *Typographic design* (Benn). A comprehensive study of the background to the subject.

RÖTTGER *Creative paper craft* (Batsford). Exercises in basic design with some immediate applications to print.

ROWLAND *Looking and seeing* series (Ginn). Nos 1 to 3: *Pattern and shape, The development of shape* and *The shapes we need* outline simply and clearly the bases of good contemporary design and are essential reading to anyone engaged in a design field.

RÜDER *Typography* (Tiranti). A superb outline of the methods of the Swiss school of typography, based on constructivist art principles. Not for the beginner, but obligatory reading for the already proficient designer.

SAUSMAREZ *Basic design* (Studio Vista). The theory of basic design, together with suggestions for a practical approach. Certain chapters are of direct help to the typographer, but the whole book should be read.

SCOTT *Design fundamentals* (McGraw-Hill). A particularly logical study of basic design, founded on perception psychology, with exercises for the student.

SELLERS *Doing it in style* (Pergamon). Though primarily for journalists, it offers a sound, unacademic approach to copy preparation which is strongly recommended to designers.

SIMON *Introduction to typography* (Faber). Compulsory reading as a guide to details of text setting and book typography.

SLOANE *Colour: basic principles and new directions* (Studio Vista). Concise statement of the contemporary attitude to colour in art and design.

SMITH *Student handbook of colour* (Reinhold). Unusually successful relation of the facts of colour perception to the creative process, with suggestions for exercises.

SPENCER *Design in business printing* (Sylvan Press) out of print. Useful guide to the elements of good typography, with special reference to stationery, by a well-known designer.

SPENCER *Pioneers of modern typography* (Lund Humphries). This book would be remarkable for the specimens it reproduces alone, but new light is shed on the period and the persons in a number of articles.

SPENCER *The visible word* (Lund Humphries). A designer looks at the whole problem of legibility.

STONE, ECKSTEIN *Preparing art for printing* (Reinhold). The tools, processes and methods of preparing artwork and photographs for reproduction.

SWANN *Techniques of typography* (Lund Humphries). Well-presented information mainly about methods of typesetting and their effects on layout.

TAYLOR *Colour technology* (Oxford). Deals primarily with the science of colour but also provides a concise summary of other aspects of colour theory and prints certain information difficult to find elsewhere.

THOMAS *The visible persuaders* (Hutchinson). Good background reading on advertising aims and methods.

TSCHICHOLD *Asymmetric typography* (Faber). A classic statement of the historical situation which led to the modern style in typography.

TURNBULL, BAIRD *The graphics of communication* (Holt, Rinehart & Winston, New York). Treats comprehensively print processes, materials and the various skills involving the designer which are required in production, such as copy preparation, layout and presentation, preparing artwork and photographs for reproduction.

WILLIAMSON *Methods of book design* (Oxford). The standard text and reference book on the subject of traditional design of books. Indispensable.

WILLS *Fundamentals of layout* (Oak Tree Press). Concerned almost solely with advertising, but with much good practical advice and information.

WILSON *The design of books* (Studio Vista). Another point of view on the subject to add to those of Williamson and Lee.

WINGLER *The Bauhaus* (MIT Press). This monumental collection of documents and photographs is the most important work on the subject.

ZACHRISSON *Legibility of printed text* (Almqvist & Wiksell, Stockholm). The most recent study of typography from the psychological point of view.

A number of other titles which
will be found useful for reference
either factual or visual

Certain other publications
not classified as books
contain information
useful to the designer of print

BRINKLEY *Lettering today* (Studio Vista)

GERSTNER, KUTTER *New graphic art* (Tiranti)

GLAISTER *Glossary of the book* (Allen & Unwin)

HEWITT *Style for print* (Blandford)

LEWIS *Printed ephemera* (Cowell)

LEWIS *The twentieth-century printed book* (Studio Vista).

MORISON, DAY *The printed book 1450–1935* (Benn)

Ad 1: an international survey of press advertising (Thames & Hudson)

Design and art direction annual (Studio Vista)

Designers in Britain (Deutsch)

The design of forms in government departments (HMSO)

Encyclopedia of type faces (Blandford)

Estimating for printers (British Federation of Master Printers)

Graphis annual (Graphis Press, Zurich)

Modern publicity annual (Studio Vista)

Penrose annual (Lund Humphries)

Typomundus 20 (Reinhold/Studio Vista)

Who's who in graphic art (Graphis Press, Zurich)

Going metric with the printing industry
Guide to book production practice
International paper sizes
Preliminary course in printing
Preparation of artwork for gravure
Preparation of artwork for offset
(British Federation of Master Printers)

Trimmed sizes of writing paper and certain classes of printed matter (ISO/R216)

Layout of periodicals (ISO/R8)

Proof correction and copy preparation (BS 1219:1958)

Specification for sizes and recommended layouts of commercial forms (BS 1808:1963)

Sizes of posters (BS 3047:1958)

Glossary of paper, stationery and allied terms (BS 3202:1964)

Guide to the selection of processes for reproducing drawings (BS 4212:1967)

The preparation of trade literature for the building industry (The Building Centre)

The Post Office Guide (GPO)

Type behaviour
A grammar of type ornament
Filmsetting in focus
(Monotype Corporation)

Photo-engraving—a beginner's guide (Pictorial Machinery Ltd)

The print user's guide to colour (Krisson Printing Ltd)

Paper and print periodical (Lund Humphries)

Graphis periodical (Graphis Press, Zurich)

Gebrauchsgraphik periodical (Bruckmann, Munich)

Monotype newsletter and *Monotype recorder* (Monotype Corporation)

Motif periodical (Shenval Press)